CERTIFIABLE

FOREWORD BY **REBECCA VAN BERGEN,**
FOUNDER AND EXECUTIVE DIRECTOR OF NEST

CHRIS VAN BERGEN

CERTIFIABLE

HOW BUSINESSES OPERATIONALIZE
RESPONSIBLE SOURCING

WILEY

Library of Congress Cataloging-in-Publication Data is Available:

ISBN 9781119890294 (Cloth)
ISBN 9781119890300 (ePub)
ISBN 9781119890317 (ePDF)

Cover Design: Chris Wallace
Cover Images: Cardboard Texture © kyoshino / Getty Images, Environmental Icons © lborg / Getty Images, Core Values Icons © -VICTOR- / Getty Images
Author Photo: courtesy of Chris Van Bergen

SKY10049669_062323

This book is dedicated to all those who are willing to ask the right questions and do the work to seek the answers: whether you are a consumer looking to make choices that align with your values, a student seeking to understand the future of business, or someone who is working from inside a firm to make change, I hope you see this book as an open doorway leading to your individual pursuit of impact.

Contents

Foreword

IN EARLY 2020, as businesses and borders began shutting down in response to the COVID-19 pandemic, my team at Nest began receiving panicked phone calls from around the world. Retailers, who were reeling from government-mandated store closures and the impending shock to their bottom lines, were cancelling orders from the factories and production partners who relied on them for revenue. As a result, the home-based craft workers and independent artisans we work with—workers who make up an essential but often invisible part of the global supply chain—had lost their primary source of income. Since many of these workers live paycheck-to-paycheck in the same developing (i.e. poor) countries that COVID hit the hardest, this disruption was not just a nuisance, but a potential catastrophe for them and their families.

Our goal at Nest has always been to support these workers by giving them the tools and resources necessary to improve their quality of life. We do that, in part, by connecting them directly with the brands who source their products. In this way, the people responsible for making sourcing decisions gain a deeper understanding of the impact they have on individual workers—often women who use their wages to supplement their family's meager income—on the other side of the world.

Now that these brands were facing massive budget shortfalls, where could we find the capital necessary to keep our homeworkers solvent? Even the most socially conscious brands couldn't afford to keep their short-term commitments without risking their long-term business model. There was no way to know how consumers would respond or when stores could reopen. We needed a creative solution, and fast.

That solution came not from the well-resourced, MBA-trained executives at our corporate brand partners but from the homeworker community itself. I called Ming-Ming Tung-Edelman, founder of the Refugee Artisan Initiative (RAI) in Seattle and one of Nest's longtime artisan partners, to see how she was faring in the midst of this unprecedented crisis. RAI helps refugee women start home-based businesses and earn a living wage by using the craft skills they've brought from their home countries. Typically, these women make piecework textiles—things like tote bags, napkins, and garments—that RAI's corporate partners commission directly. Within days of Seattle announcing its city-wide shutdowns, they had pivoted to making masks for use in city hospitals and government agencies. The dozen women RAI employed were working as quickly as they could, but they could never meet the demand on their own. That's when a light bulb went off. What if we could find a way to pay our network of craft workers—many of whom were skilled sewers and were used to working in the safety of their own homes—to fill this gap?

We organized meetings with some of our key brand partners, and within three weeks Nest had raised more than $1 million. Over the next three months this money would fund the production of hand-sewn PPE for essential workers in 18 countries, 92 hospitals, and 47 community organizations, including the United States Postal Service and New York City Housing Authority. All told, the effort saved 4,580 artisan jobs.

As I write this, exactly three years later, I realize the lessons we learned from this experience are just as, if not more, applicable today. COVID-19 reshaped the way we think about a lot of things: how we work, how we take care of ourselves and one another, how we interact, how reliable our governments and institutions are in times of crisis, and how we spend our time. For many, it also revealed something we at Nest have known for the almost two decades we've been around: the importance of reliable, sustainable, and agile supply chains for maintaining our way of life.

While production has mostly returned to pre-pandemic levels, disruptions to the supply chain have only become more frequent and noticeable. In the past three years, consumers have found themselves, at various points, unable to access baby formula, tampons, eggs, gasoline, vaccines, electronics (due to a shortage in the raw materials used to make the microchips that power them), and other items they once took for granted. Globalization has made our economy more dependent on complex and diffuse supply chains without providing the systems necessary to ensure transparency, accountability, and resilience within them. Without this capacity, the global economy remains vulnerable—to pandemics, to political turmoil, to environmental disasters, and to any other forces outside our control.

Corporations and governments are finally waking up to the need to address these insecurities. But because they have, for decades, largely ceded responsibility for this issue to those who work closer to the source, they often lack the insight and resources necessary to know where to start. We at Nest are proud to work with these organizations by getting them to do a conceptually simple but practically radical thing: talk to the individuals who actually make their products. By connecting them with the home-based independent artisan craft workers—whether they're RAI's refugee workers in Seattle, rug weavers in India, or brass casters in Kenya—we help them better understand the role they play, not just in their own organizations, but in the global economy as a whole. The result is not just a feel-good story of interpersonal connection and humanitarian perspective but a shift toward a more socially conscious and environmentally sustainable way of thinking that considers the impact of a business's decisions well beyond its bottom line.

My husband and business partner's book is an attempt to bring the experience we create for our partners at Nest to the largest audience possible. It shows exactly how supply chains have evolved—for better and worse—since the industrial age and examines both the challenges and the opportunities companies face when deciding how to move forward in our intricate, ever-changing, and uncertain world. It forces leaders to reckon with the choices they make and ask themselves what sort of legacy they want to have. Do they want to be known for record-breaking profits or technological innovation? Or do they want to consider how their decisions affect people they may never meet in places they may never visit? Is it possible they could be known for both?

The beauty in Chris's book is in how it makes the case that businesses no longer have to choose. Sustainability, responsible sourcing, and ethical business practices are no longer in conflict with profitability and competitive advantage. If anything, they are imperative to it. I hope that, by reading this book, you will walk away both educated and inspired, ready to use your voice or your power, both within your organization or as a consumer, to help us build a more prosperous and resilient future for all.

—Rebecca van Bergen
Found and Executive Director, Nest
March 2023

1

Down the Dusty Road: The Complexity of Supply Chains in the Age of Globalization

". . .Two roads diverged in a wood, and I—I took the one less traveled by, And that has made all the difference."
                                    —From "The Road Not Taken" by Robert Frost

IT HAS ALREADY been a long day—rewarding, but exhausting—by the time we arrive for our last interview. As I get out of the car, my shirt sticks to my back with sweat, a result of the afternoon heat and humidity in this part of the Philippines. I'm in the Pampanga Province, an area northwest of Manila, outside a simple cinderblock home with a corrugated metal roof. I survey the landscape around me. Chickens saunter slowly across the dirt road, and I can hear a goat bleating from somewhere within the courtyard of the home I'm about to enter. Subsistence crops grow to one side; wildflowers grow on the other. My job has taken me on countless trips just like this one all around the world, and yet I take a moment to appreciate why I'm here. Within that courtyard, next to the noisy goat and perhaps a scurrying cat or two, sits one of the world's hundreds of millions of home-based workers. The woman I am about to visit makes products that will wind up on the shelves of stores in the United States and across Europe before finding their way into the homes of consumers who may not even know she exists.

In the more than 10 years I have worked within and observed global supply chains, I've conducted hundreds of interviews like the ones we are doing today. My two travel companions, however, are still new to these sorts of environments. They are here to represent their employer, a large, publicly traded, multi-billion-dollar brand with thousands of stores across the United States known for its commitment to accessible price points for its customers. Sourcing the thousands of products that appear on store shelves is not an easy road to navigate, which is why we're here. My companions work for the team responsible for making sure the products owned by the brand (i.e. not purchased from an outside company such as Johnson

3

& Johnson or PepsiCo) are produced and sourced in line with the company's supplier code of conduct. Does the production of this product have positive or negative impacts for the world at large? Are workers treated and compensated fairly at all points in the supply chain? What is the environmental impact of production? How does production impact the surrounding communities? My companions are the eyes and ears of the brand. They, like me, travel wherever production is happening and serve as a conduit of information and best practices to a multitude of other teams within the company whose hands help bring a product to market.

Most major brands have some type of supplier code—a set of broad, often vague, rules designed to articulate how the brand expects its suppliers to behave and how it intends to hold itself accountable. Unfortunately, they are not exactly an instruction manual, and it is behind these codes of conduct that the real work (and complexity) begins.

Retailers typically consider it sufficient for third-party suppliers (such as Johnson & Johnson and PepsiCo) to show proof of various certifications or make specific commitments about their behavior. The retailer itself rarely looks further into those supply chains since they are the supplier's responsibility. However, with products that the brand or retailer fully owns themselves, such as the ones my travel buddies oversee, there is a lot more at stake: the brand designs and commissions these products, but they typically outsource production to a factory overseas. That means they don't have direct control over how their products are produced. For brands that pride themselves on being good corporate citizens and having a positive impact on their stakeholders, this poses a significant risk. When you're sourcing products from all corners of the globe, how do you ensure they're sourced responsibly? That is the central question of this book.

The Opportunities and Challenges of Responsible Sourcing

Throughout my career, I have had first-hand experience in the work it takes to bring responsibly sourced products to market. For the past 11 years, I have worked as the chief financial and operations officer at Nest, a nonprofit founded in 2006 to help home-based and artisan makers from around the world grow their businesses sustainably and ethically. As part of my role, I work closely with brands and corporations to help them navigate their complex global supply chains to ensure they are operating in line with their stated goals and values. The result? Companies are able to make better decisions that support the myriad actors throughout their supply chains: from the owner of a massive factory in Shandong Province, China, to the weaver in Huancayo, Peru, who works from their kitchen table. Combined with my experience teaching in some of the top business programs in the United States, I have witnessed the powerful impact created when brands prioritize ethical sourcing practices and get their strategy right.

But no matter how hard companies try to smooth out the kinks in their supply chains, there will always be something they miss or do not anticipate. Thanks to globalization and technology, supply chains have become so complex that it's harder than ever to *really* know what's going on at all levels. At the same time, consumer behavior and the rapid spread of information have made it even more important to pay attention to these things. If you do not, you could lose customers—and your actions could have disastrous ripple effects for the populations with whom you work. How do you try and prevent the problems? Whose responsibility is it? How should a brand react and address the issue? And how do they balance the expectations of all their stakeholders—their board and CEO, their managers and co-workers, their customers, investors, and the production partners themselves? If you work within one of these firms, how can you increase the positive impacts that your company (or your career) is creating? As an investor or consumer, how do you evaluate the behavior or promises of your favorite companies when you do not actually know what it means to put those promises into action? What do all those little symbols and certifications printed on your favorite brand's labels and packaging really mean, anyway?

Nest and the World of Handcraft

This trip to Pampanga is the first stop in a two-week jaunt across Southeast Asia and offers a glimpse into some of the challenges and opportunities brands face when it comes to ethical sourcing. I'm here as part of the pilot for Nest's revolutionary supply chain transparency program,[1] which we designed as a way for our corporate partners to gain greater understanding of and appreciation for the complexity inherent in sourcing handmade, artisan products from around the globe. Around the world, millions of artisans and craft workers—most of them women—produce handmade goods—often from within their homes—that are then sold to brands and, eventually, consumers. Our work at Nest involves bringing brands into contact with these craft workers, often for the first time, so that all parties in the supply chain can better understand their roles and responsibilities to one another. This is really important since this is not currently typical in the industry. According to a sequence of surveys issued by Nest alongside GLG (Gerson Lehrman Group), only 4% of brands report that they are always conducting home visits when it comes to assessing work beyond the factory,[2] so very few are getting complete transparency to the individuals in their homes who are performing handwork, thus stunting their knowledge base—and ultimately their ability to create solutions. This visit to the Philippines is a big moment for the program. I am here to assess how well a production vendor has been able to stand up a viable compliance program that reaches their homeworkers based on the training and resources Nest has previously provided. It is a task made even larger considering that this particular supply chain employs hundreds, if not thousands, of basket weavers over multiple islands in the region.

Basket weaving, as it is with most craft businesses, grew out of necessity and ingenuity. In Pampanga, locals started weaving baskets from vines commonly found in nearby jungles as a way to store things in their own homes. Over time, the practice expanded as the baskets became an exportable, mass-produced, handmade product and, eventually, a booming business in the Philippines, Indonesia, and China, as well as many regions in Africa such as Rwanda, Uganda, Ghana, and Kenya. Skills, techniques, designs, and materials vary from region to region and sometimes from weaver to weaver. If you buy a handmade basket from your local home goods store, chances are, it was produced in a similar place to the one we are about to enter. Not a factory but a home. Not made by machine but crafted by skilled hands working at lightning speed even during this hot afternoon. (And even when that basket is from a low-cost retailer where the goods might all appear to be machine-made!)

In the distance we can still hear faint strains of the cacophony of the central square in the main town we drove through a few minutes before. There, street vendors sell their wares in the shadow of an old Spanish cathedral. Cars and motorbikes zig this way and that through the bustling streets. Out here, it is quiet. I can hear a rooster in the yard and music coming from somewhere behind the house. We open the gate and walk through, making our way into a courtyard where we find the source of the music. On the far side of the courtyard stands a newer building with cement floors. A woman sits next to it, listening to a radio as she deftly weaves a basket through her expert fingers. Wire frames, the skeleton for this type of basket, sit on one side of the building. Completed baskets sit on the other. The woman looks up and smiles. She's been expecting us ever since her point of contact at the production company let her know we were going to stop by sometime today.

Laurie, the Personification of a Global Supply Chain

We introduce ourselves to the woman and learn that her name is Laurie. As we talk, she never stops weaving, winding and tying a vine-like rope around the wire frame. Laurie smiles and invites us to sit next to her on a few mismatched plastic chairs. My companions and I situate ourselves, and I begin the interview. Laurie tells us she has been weaving for more than 10 years, since her mid-30s, and that we are standing in her workshop, which she built with part of her earnings. Before she became a basket weaver, she had been a domestic worker—a common occupation for many within her community—first in Singapore and then in Dubai. She returned to her community because she missed her family. She wanted to be close to raise her daughters and care for her elderly mother, and basket weaving has enabled her to do just that. Laurie had not really engaged in the craft when she was younger, but upon her return to the village other family members took her under their wing and trained her. Research has shown that when the women of a household earn income, they invariably use it to feed, clothe, and support their children and families.[3] Laurie is no exception. In addition to building her workshop, Laurie has used her earnings to maintain her home and pay for her children to attend school. She beams with pride as she informs us that her daughter is about to start nursing school, making her the first in the family to earn an education beyond high school. Laurie is not the sole breadwinner. Her husband has a motorcycle and works as an occasional informal taxi driver for local travelers. As he naps on a hammock nearby, Laurie chuckles. "Now that I'm working and earning money on my own,

I've become *his* boss!" she says. "He helps me make baskets. He's not as good as me, but I'm helping him get better." It is very clear who is in charge here, and it is definitely not the man snoring in the hammock.

As we continue the interview, Laurie confirms the seemingly impossible journey her baskets take on their way to a shelf in the United States. She works with a local village leader, who distributes the work between Laurie and the other weavers in her community. Laurie is paid a set rate for each basket she completes—standard practice known as "piece-rate" for this type of work as opposed to an hourly wage. Each week, the village leader picks up all the baskets from the various weavers and gets them ready for a subcontractor from the region. The subcontractor picks up the completed baskets (often tying them together 10 to 15 high on the back of a motorcycle) while dropping off the raw materials for the next week's orders. That subcontractor puts the full set of completed baskets on the back of a small truck, which makes its way to a finishing factory for final quality inspections, varnishing, and packaging. (It's at facilities like this one where brand representatives like the ones I'm traveling with usually start their inquiries into a supply chain.) From there, the baskets are taken by truck, then boat, to a distribution center in the United States where they wait for final delivery to the store and eventually into the homes of the consumer. We ask Laurie how she is treated by the village leader, and she tells us what we hoped. He treats her well, pays her on time, and has never harassed or abused her.

The interview is winding down, and I offer the brand team an opportunity to engage with Laurie directly. Up to this point they have been playing the role of observer on the trip, but they are clearly interested in interacting directly with a woman who represents part of the supply chain they have never been able to see before. Their work takes them onto the factory floor, but never to remote village communities such as this, or to workers with such an interesting story. They ask if Laurie knows where they are from, or where her baskets go when she is done with them. She laughs and says she's always wondered about that, though she's just happy to have the work. When one of the brand representatives tells her who they work for, her face lights up. "Do you mean to tell me that there are people in New York City who have my basket in their house?" Now it's the brand team member's turn to laugh. Turns out, she has that same basket in her own home. Laurie, with a gleam in her eye, says that if she saw a picture, she might be able to tell us if it was one of hers. "We all have our secret tricks," she says. "Looking at a basket you can tell if the weaver was left-handed or right-handed." The brand representative tells her she doesn't have a photo on her but will be sure to send an image of the basket once she returns home.

An Unexpected Question from Laurie

As our time with Laurie comes to an end, one of the brand reps asks if there is anything else Laurie would like the team to know. Laurie says this is the first time anyone has ever asked her these types of questions. It's certainly the first time she has ever met anyone from the brand that buys her product. She expresses her gratitude for the work and says she loves the thought of someone from the other side of the globe appreciating her craft. But then, for the first time since our arrival, Laurie's hands pause at her basket. She looks into the faces of the two brand representatives and asks, "Why has the price I get paid for this basket never gone up in 10 years? The cost of living has increased, and the minimum wage has gone up at least three times, but I get paid the same." Later, after we've had time to assess the matter further, we learn that minimum wage in the region has actually gone up four times since Laurie started weaving, and the cost of living has increased over 3% on average each year during that same period.[4] Yet Laurie still gets paid the same amount per basket that she did 10 years ago. This is the first time that a brand has heard directly from a worker like Laurie, and now they are learning about an issue they were not previously aware of but were inadvertently complicit in. Laure's inquiry raised a bigger question: What role does a brand play in creating downstream impacts (either positive or negative)? In this case, since the brand had not increased its cost per product in the last 10 years, it would stand to reason that worker wages would not have increased. In a traditional sourcing model, the brand and production vendor enter into business negotiations regarding how much they will pay for a finished piece, but the brand does not know how much of that price goes to the workers. Factory workers are usually salaried employees, not piece-rate ones like Laurie and other homeworkers. As a result, brands can verify their vendors are paying at least minimum wage salaries in an audit. From the brand's perspective, any negotiation that takes place would therefore have little impact on worker wages and instead only affect the amount of margin each party takes per product. In fact, when brands renegotiate their contracts with existing vendors, they typically try to *decrease* the price they pay per unit, assuming the factories operate more efficiently at a larger scale. They fail to consider how this downward price pressure might impact workers like Laurie because these workers sit outside of the audited factory. And yet, the amount they pay to their factory partners directly impacts how much those partners can pay their subcontractors, and eventually home-based workers, deeper into the supply chain.

Laurie's simple question perfectly highlights the challenges brands face when trying to behave responsibly. What can we learn when we look deeper into the supply chain? The issue of verifying fair wages alone is an important one. A surprising 79% of the supply chains we work with at Nest were not able to demonstrate that they meet minimum wage when we first start working together, yet nearly 40% have closed the gap within a year of participating in our Ethical Handcraft Program, and 65% have implemented measures to do so over the course of the next year. These findings highlight that third-party accountability and standardization of wage-setting processes are critical. In Laurie's case, giving her a voice created a dramatically positive ripple effect, as solutions for proper wages involve both the producer business and their partnering brand.

The Journey This Book Will Take

But this light bulb moment in the Philippines is just one example of what you can uncover when you start looking closer. Replace "baskets" with virtually any product from coffee to clothing to diamonds, and you will face the same issues that our brand partner did. As you work through this book, we will explore the shifting corporate philosophy and behavior regarding responsibility. We will explore the history of globalization and how increased complexity of the supply chain led to the increase in expectation around corporate behavior, looking at a few key moments that served as particular turning points. We will walk through the internal and external forces at play that impact decision making when it comes to responsible sourcing and how companies are rethinking the nature of their sourcing relationships in order to shift from a short-term, combative mentality to a longer-term, supportive one that enables collaboration and problem solving. As a result of the need for visibility and accountability, we will look at the world of compliance standards, certification systems, and auditing. We will look at how the auditing experience itself has changed for the better: no longer with vendors trying to hide issues out of fear of losing business but instead in uncovering the reasons why issues may be occurring in the first place. We will also look into what, tragically, can happen when that auditing and compliance system breaks down. We will explore the ways brands and corporations are investing in innovations to drive increased transparency and impact; the rise in authentic messaging to consumers, investors, and employees; the role of finance in this whole equation; and fundamentally how supply chain responsibility is leveraged both as a risk mitigation tool *and* a business driver for firms.

A Successful Trip

Our work in the Philippines was an all-around success: the Nest program was able to help this basket-weaving business establish strong compliance systems within their complicated supply chain, and through the process our brand partner established a closer linkage to the people making their product, which resulted in positive impacts for the wages of all the workers. But it also highlighted some of the challenges to sourcing products from the four corners of the world: there is always the potential to uncover a new issue. And it is this complexity, and opportunity, that this book is all about.

Welcome to corporate responsibility and sourcing in the 21st century.

2

Globalization and a Corporate Crisis

"Life is divided into three terms—that which was, which is, and which will be. Let us learn from the past to profit by the present, and from the present, to live better in the future."

— William Wordsworth

"The past can hurt. But the way I see it, you can either run from it, or learn from it."

— Walt Disney

ONE HUNDRED YEARS ago, the idea of a corporate executive from the United States meeting face-to-face with the woman weaving baskets for the company in her home in the Philippines would have been straight out of science fiction. But the rise of globalization has made the world interconnected in ways no one living at the turn of the 20th century could have imagined. Designers have access to new materials and techniques; if they can think it, chances are someone, somewhere can produce it. Consumers expect their cherished goods to be in ready supply at whatever brick-and-mortar or online store they shop at and on their doorstep days, if not hours, later. When that is not possible, there's a problem (save for disruptions such as global pandemics). Thanks to increased competition, production companies feel more pressure to create products in record time, in higher quality, with faster delivery, and with more innovation than ever before. As a result, people like our basket weaver Laurie are able to benefit from newfound economic opportunity, a chance to remain in their community and be productive to support their family. When the system works, it encourages a race to the top. More work, more wages, more innovation, better products, and stronger economies overall.

However, if the system lacks standards of ethics and greed goes unchecked, history has proven there will be few winners and many losers. Within the traditional sourcing model, the corporate motivation to pursue profit above all else has historically led to a race to the

17

bottom. Companies chase the lowest cost for the highest return with no regard for or loyalty to the producer. On a constant quest for the best return, companies pit vendors against each other, leading to issues—sometimes abuses—within the supply chain. The company, facing pressures around profit from investors or board members, turns a blind eye and lets questions go unanswered. Limited transparency breeds a diminished sense of ownership and responsibility, creating the perfect environment for worker and environmental exploitation. To use a stark example, slavery has existed since the dawn of recorded history. And still today—the most prosperous era the world has ever known—there are people toiling under this vile practice, suffering due to corporate greed or neglect. The use of forced labor has been linked to the Uyghur population in the Xinjiang Province in China within the cotton supply chain, and many of our electronics are produced with minerals pulled from mines in the Democratic Republic of Congo via forced labor.[1] It is not just the abuse of the global workforce; overconsumption and massively complex supply chains are degrading our planet from deforestation to the carbon required to ship things around the globe.

Who Is to Blame?

An easy target to blame for this misbehavior is Milton Friedman, a name you probably recognize if you have ever taken any business-related coursework. Friedman was an economist whose 1970 essay "A Friedman Doctrine: The Social Responsibility of Business Is to Increase Its Profits"[2] continues to influence business leaders today. In the piece, Friedman argued that, just as the title declares, a corporation's *sole* purpose is to increase returns to its shareholders. Furthermore, any activity that does not actively increase those profits, including those related to corporate responsibility, is equivalent to stealing money right out of shareholders' pockets. Even today, despite the threats of climate change, a global pandemic, and calls for greater equality, many business leaders still tout (even if subconsciously) Friedman's philosophy as gospel. Think about the car manufacturer that makes claims their diesel engine is better for the environment without having the research and data to in fact support these claims (Volkswagen), or the financial institution that develops a program of issuing credit cards customers didn't ask for in order to boost loan numbers at the expense of hard-working lower income and middle class families (Wells Fargo), or the countless companies that make claims of caring for their customers but launch aggressive anti-union campaigns against their employees. The leaders at these companies use Friedman's philosophy to excuse such behavior.

But this is not a book about the evil of corporations, the flaws of capitalism, or the downsides of globalization. In fact, I, along with many other socially minded people in business, actually agree with aspects of Friedman's premise: but I give it a modern twist. A corporation does, indeed, have an obligation to provide profits to its shareholders. Otherwise, it would be, or should be, a nonprofit organization or government agency, which exist to serve the public good (and as an executive for a nonprofit, I do see the value in those). However, the for-profit firm *also* has a responsibility to its shareholders to adapt and change to maintain its existence, and within the existence of society, in perpetuity. If in the course of doing business, a company is actively harming the environment or the people making or consuming its products, it is not acting in its own best interest (let alone that of the society around it). In a world of mounting environmental concerns, global pandemics, and increased social unrest, corporations need to not only limit their negative externalities but actively produce positive impacts. It is out of these ideas that the concepts of regenerative finance, conscious capitalism, stakeholder engagement, and, yes, responsible sourcing have taken root and come into public consciousness. And here is the kicker: data is now starting to prove that if a company pursues profit *and* a more socially minded purpose, it becomes better able to absorb market shocks (such as COVID-19) and is more likely to increase above-market returns for its shareholders over the long term. In its 2019 report, the Torrey Project found that ethical companies (using the 48 US companies listed by Ethisphere on their Ethical Companies List,[3] 18 companies listed in the book *Firms of Endearment*,[4] and the nine actively traded companies from the book *Good to Great*[5]) experienced stock price growth of 50% more than the S&P 500 when looking at performance over the last 20 years.[6] What do you think Friedman would have to say about that?

If we assume corporations have a responsibility toward their employees, consumers, suppliers, and larger communities, the question becomes what *kind* of responsibility? How far does it extend? Since this is a book focused on sourcing and supply chains, I'll leave the arguments about government control of worker protections, employee wages, taxes, and other worthy concerns for another book. But that still leaves plenty of questions for us to explore. As our world becomes more complicated and interconnected, how can companies exercise their responsibility and how far does that responsibility extend? What factors do they need to consider? And how do they maintain visibility when they quite literally may have never seen where their goods are being produced? Those are the questions we'll continue to explore in this book.

To understand the current state of feelings regarding corporate responsibility—and to better predict where we're headed in the future—it's useful to take a minute to consider the past. How did we arrive at our current moment? How did supply chains become so vast and complex? How have the standards changed and why? And where have current feelings regarding corporate obligations come from? For me, it all starts with globalization and the dramatic decentralization of production.

The Rise of Globalization

When I think of how a community and industry can be impacted by globalization, my mind goes first to New York City's Garment District. Perhaps it's because, before the pandemic, the Nest offices were located in midtown Manhattan, just a few blocks from the one-square-mile area that was once the center of the American clothing manufacturing industry. The rise of garment trade in the area, which stretched from 34th to 42nd streets and was bordered by Fifth and Ninth Avenues, was fueled by the prevalence of cheap, immigrant labor (at a time in the early 1900s when 2,000+ people came through Ellis Island every day), combined with its geographic proximity to the wealthy factory owners. Keep in mind that telephone lines only started appearing in New York City in the 1880s, so the easiest way for an owner to know what was happening on the line was to go visit in person. With access to a large working port for both raw materials and for the distribution of finished products, the Garment District once housed 450 textile factories and employed more than 40,000 people.

Today the area looks vastly different. Yes, some fabric and trim shops still exist, but the number and types of businesses have changed dramatically. Gone are the mass-manufacturing operations, replaced now by specialist businesses that are much fewer in number. Some businesses, such as M&S Schmalberg,[7] founded in 1916, continue to survive by making significant pivots. Now a fourth-generation business, it is the last remaining silk-flower manufacturer in New York City, which once housed more than 10. In its more than 100 years in business, M&S Schmalberg has had to shift their business model from one that produces large-quantity orders to more customized work, both for wholesale and for a growing direct-to-consumer online operation. So where did the jobs go, and why?

Global innovations around communication and transportation played a role. Think about the impact of the advent of phones, then fax machines, the Internet, and now our ability to make video calls from our phones, beaming to a satellite and landing on the other side of the globe in a matter of milliseconds. In addition, with new modes of transportation becoming available, the movement of both raw materials and finished goods has become much more efficient from both a time and a cost perspective. Ships became much larger; the largest cargo ship today is more than 1.5 times larger than the Titanic. Trains became much more efficient, shifting from coal-powered steam to diesel. And the advent of the semi-truck in 1898, eventually making its way to the 18-wheel tractor-trailer in the 1930s that today can haul 80,000 pounds when fully loaded with cargo. With the expansion of sourcing opportunities, as a result of cheaper shipping costs and lower labor costs in developing economies, businesses no longer needed to rely on the supplier next door. This impacted the Garment District in a very real way. Through the 1900s, the cost of labor in New York City started to increase alongside the steady increases in the overall cost of living as well. Both were a direct result of an increase in population and the strain of limited resources. Economy 101: the law of supply and demand. Between 1900 and 1910, the population of Manhattan grew by over 1.3 million.[8] By 1920 it had grown by another 850,000 people. Where was everyone supposed to live? What were they going to eat? And what other resources were they going to draw from? Manhattan is an island: competition for space meant rising costs of rent and operations as well. This is still seen today. Simultaneously, the growing immigrant workforce began to organize, with the first union, The International Ladies Garment Workers Union, formed in 1900.[9] By 1909 workers began to publicly express their frustration with their working conditions and wages, exemplified by the "Uprising of Twenty Thousand" led by Ukrainian immigrant Clara Lemlich, which stopped production for the period of two months.[10]

Producing in New York City was becoming less and less appealing, and when brands that traditionally sourced products from New York were presented with other alternatives, it was next to impossible for suppliers such as M&S Schmalberg to compete on price. Orders first started moving to the South, chasing lower labor and materials costs, and then out West to California, which was having an immigrant boom of its own. Finally, the work moved away to other countries, where it remains today. Looking on your hangtags, you continue to see the names of far-off places such as Bangladesh, China, Indonesia, Vietnam, or Ethiopia.

The Role of Government in Globalization

Rising costs were not the only factor that contributed to globalization. Government incentives, such as tariffs and tax incentives designed to facilitate (or limit) business transactions between countries, also encouraged corporations to start looking elsewhere. The North American Free Trade Act (NAFTA) of 1994 provides a great case study to examine the impact such policies had on jobs and local sourcing opportunities. Designed to ease business frictions between the United States, Canada, and Mexico, NAFTA has been, in many ways, a great success. NAFTA's orchestrators believed it would grow the overall US economy by 0.5% year over year by doing things such as reducing tariffs on imported goods, driving exports, and creating common standards around workplace safety, labor rights, and environmental protection.[11] The effort created almost five million new jobs to support all the resulting free-trade activities.[12] These jobs, as NAFTA's supporters point out, generally came with higher pay than the existing jobs in direct manufacturing. In addition, NAFTA created a whole new world of investment opportunities for the wealthy in both Canada and Mexico. For example, within just the first year of NAFTA's passage, foreign direct investment (FDI) in Canada grew over 400%.[13] While investors were reaping the benefits, the governments themselves were also seeing positive impacts. Government contracts were now open to businesses from any of the three countries and therefore became much more competitive, lowering the overall costs. Sounds great, right?

Well, while NAFTA created many new jobs, it also eliminated many others, including those within production communities like the Garment District, California, or the South. The lower cost of labor and the lower production facility operating costs in Mexico were simply too hard to resist. By some estimates, more than 682,000 jobs had been eliminated by 2010 as a result of NAFTA.[14]

We can see how this impacted local economies by examining one in particular. Florence, Alabama, was known as the "Cotton T-shirt Capital of the World" by the early 1980s,[15] driving the local economy in a state that held 100,000+ jobs in textile manufacturing. Following the signing of NAFTA, almost all of the factories there shuttered and sat dormant for decades until a very recent resurgence coming from slow-fashion pioneers.[16] Similar stories can be heard in California, where the overall percentage of manufacturing jobs shrunk from 16.9% to 8.9% of all employment in the state during a similar period in time.[17] For many in Mexico, NAFTA led to negative experiences as well, particularly in the farming communities. As subsidized US crops flooded the market, Mexican farmers either found themselves out of work or forced to cut corners to try and compete on price. This resulted in the rampant use of toxic fertilizers to help increase harvests as well as deforestation to clear more land for farming.[18]

Like most things in life, change can be complicated, and NAFTA was far from the only factor that spurred on globalization. Others include the United States' membership into the World Trade

Organization, currency fluctuations, and inflation. All the while, the rest of the world was simultaneously growing its production capabilities, becoming increasingly competitive. Countries in Southeast Asia were leveraging a much lower cost of living to develop labor-intensive industries such as garment manufacturing, as well as embracing skill sets, such as basket weaving, that could differentiate their products from those produced elsewhere. The world was becoming increasingly connected and intertwined from a supply chain perspective. And just as brands started seeking ever-lower cost of goods, consumers started embracing lower price tags at checkout. Even in New York City, home of the Garment District, there was less emphasis on "Made in America" and more on the price of the product. The age of ever-present discounts, and the $8 T-shirt was in full swing, an age of hyper consumerism—as exemplified by the movie *Mallrats*, an ode to consumer culture, released in 1995.

Globalization dramatically increased the availability of cheaper and more differentiated products, but it also increased the complexity of supply chains and limited the visibility into how things were being made (as well as their positive and negative impact). Sourcing in new countries and economies also opened up the need to examine cultures, values, and the quality of life in places that you may never have heard of before and in countries where government, and labor law, could be vastly varied. Suddenly there were more people and more steps between the distributor and the manufacturer. Over time, consumers started to wonder where exactly all these cheap products came from, and why they were so much less expensive than things made closer to home. It was these questions, combined with a few very public supply chain catastrophes, that started to shift societal and business expectations toward corporate responsibility.

Nike's Crisis: A Turning Point in Corporate Responsibility

In fact, just a year after the release of *Mallrats* there was a brand crisis that, in many ways, shaped both the modern consumer mentality and corporate behavior in regard to responsible sourcing: the Nike soccer ball scandal of 1996. The event itself, combined with Nike's reaction, spurred the establishment of responsible sourcing teams; interest in environmental, social, and governance (ESG) performance; and, more personally, led me to help develop Nest's Ethical Handcraft program.

It is important to discuss the scandal, but our focus here will be on *why* it happened and most importantly the resulting impact of it. In the mid-1990s, Nike was dominating the competition when it came to athleticwear and sporting goods. They were the king of celebrity endorsements, with Michael Jordan's Air Jordan shoes having launched in 1985 (by 2019, the value of this brand was estimated at $3 billion)[19] and, beyond basketball, engaging the best of the best: Tiger Woods in golf (he was the face of Nike golf as soon as he went pro in 1996), Jerry Rice in football, and countless other household names. Nike was able to pour so much money into these types of endorsements primarily because of its business model, imagined by founder Phil Knight while he was in business school in the 1960s. Since the company's inception in 1964, Nike opted to focus exclusively on design and marketing and to outsource all production of its shoes. At a time when just 4% of all shoes were imported, this decision was revolutionary.[20] Now termed "Nikefication" by Gerald Davis in his book *The Vanishing American Corporation*,[21] this model of a "virtual corporation" has been replicated across industries, from fashion to pharmaceuticals to technology. There is a reason that your Apple iPhone comes in a case that says, "Designed in California." *Designed* but not *produced* there. If a company is not burdened with the operating costs of running its own manufacturing, it can indeed spend more money than competitors on marketing and innovation. And, as an added benefit, it puts the brand in the driver's seat when getting its contracted producers to compete on price.

Shortly after graduating from Stanford's business school, Knight partnered with a business in Japan to start producing their best-selling athletic shoes. From there, Nike production bounced all over Asia: first Japan, then South Korea, China, and Taiwan. As economies in these countries of production became more established, Nike tended to shift its focus elsewhere (chasing the lowest price) landing in China, then Indonesia and Vietnam.[22] While Nike's innovative and high design shoes require a degree of production sophistication, they were more open for other items. For less-complicated products, such as soccer balls, they sought production in less-developed economies, such as Pakistan.

Can you see the risk developing here? If a corporation is motivated solely by the lowest cost of production, combined with the fact that they do not own the production directly, how low are they willing to go when it comes to the pay and conditions of the workers making the shoes? For all its benefits, this operating model added significant risk to Nike's supply chain, since in a quest to find the lowest-cost producer Nike was decreasing its own visibility into its full supply chain—and, with every move to a new country of production, opening more unknowns. As early as 1991, labor activists such as Jeff Ballinger started trying to raise awareness of the poor conditions and wages that existed in the factories of Nike's production partners. In 1992, Ballinger published an article in *Harper's Magazine* that highlighted the issue of wages, providing the actual paystub of a worker in a Nike-contracted facility.[23] It demonstrated that the labor cost to manufacture an $80 pair of shoes was a paltry 12 cents. Further, Ballinger compared the lucrative endorsement contract of Michael Jordan to this worker, showing that it would take the worker 44,492 years to earn the same amount. Perhaps not the fairest comparison, given the brand value provided by Jordan and the massive difference in the cost of living between the two countries, but it still made a very strong statement. Still, it wasn't until 1996 that Nike's departure from vertically integrated production to a fully outsourced model became a major public relations crisis.

That year, *Life Magazine* published an expose on the use of child labor throughout the global supply chain.[24] The article, titled "Six Cents an Hour," mentioned several industries, including rugs, brick-making, and surgical equipment. But the writer placed particular emphasis on soccer-ball production in Pakistan and mentioned Nike by name. In fact, the primary image accompanying the article featured a young boy—clearly a child—hand-sewing a soccer ball emblazoned with the Nike "swoosh." Here was a beloved American brand, one that provides sporting equipment to adults and children alike, with the most recognizable marketing campaigns in the world, being implicated in a wide network of child labor production related to the fastest growing youth sport in the country. Nike had to respond. Its approach, however, did nothing to quell the growing outrage. Within the article itself, Nike spokeswoman Donna Gibbs acknowledged that Nike had yet to do anything to eliminate child labor from its supply chain. "[Child labor] is an ages-old practice, and the process of change is going to take time," said Gibbs. "Too often well-intentioned human rights groups can cause dramatic negative effects if they scare companies into stopping production, and the kids are thrown out on the street."[25] It is a complicated issue to be sure, and to remove children from this situation without a plan would cause additional negative impacts. But for the company to acknowledge that they were doing nothing to resolve it? Weren't they ethically, if not legally, obligated to do *something*? Actually, from a legal perspective, Nike was completely in the clear here. Over the 20th century, American labor law had evolved to outlaw child labor and require that companies provide safe and humane working conditions and fair wage practices to its workers. However, no law on the books held companies responsible for the workers in *contracted* facilities.

Legal risk was one thing, but consumer reaction was another. The bad press moved beyond the readership of *Harper's* and *Life* and into late night television, the big screen, and the comics. The popular comic strip *Doonesbury* devoted a week to taking swipes at the brand, featuring a storyline where a Vietnamese American character visits her cousin in a Nike factory in Vietnam where workers utter phrases like "I cannot even afford to eat."[26] "It's so hot out I am sweating like a 10 year-old Malaysian kid in a Nike factory," joked Jay Leno on *The Tonight Show*,[27] and filmmaker Michael Moore featured his hard-edged interview with Nike co-founder and CEO Phil Knight in his documentary *The Big One*.[28] The issue was truly front and center in the public consciousness, and the outrage spread to college campuses, where students organized boycotts of Nike products that resulted in Nike losing its sportswear deals with the athletic teams there. Protestors showed up to grand openings of new Nike stores around the country, staging events that were covered by papers from coast to coast. "Just Don't Do It" read one of the more popular signs carried by the activists.[29]

Nike Creates a Shift in the Industry

The onslaught on Nike's reputation soon began to impact its performance at the register. In 1998, Nike lost revenue for the first time in 13 years. After taking a hard look in the mirror (and listening to stockholder concerns), Nike leadership created a road map for a new level of brand responsibility, laying the groundwork for modern-day corporate social responsibility (CSR). No longer could these issues be brushed off as the efforts of "well-intentioned human rights groups," as Donna Gibbs had referred to them in the *Life Magazine* article. The market itself was signaling its interest in the issues by voting with consumer dollars. On May 13, 1998, Phil Knight in his role as Nike's chairman and chief executive, announced that Nike was taking responsibility for the conditions and child labor concerns in all factories that produced Nike products around the world.[30] They raised their accepted minimum age of workers to 18 (the international standard is 15), implemented stronger standards around health and safety—demanding that factories meet the US standards instead of those of their own country—and opened the door for increased transparency by enabling labor and human rights groups to join the independent auditors that observed factory conditions. The company became a leading member of the Fair Labor Organization (FLA), a multilateral organization that involves industry members, government, and labor-rights activists in order to set standards for working conditions around the world. Additionally, Nike began utilizing philanthropy to improve worker well-being, providing factory workers capital they could use for agriculture and other side businesses, as well as creating entrepreneurship programs to help these budding side enterprises. As Knight declared in his statement to the press, "We believe that these are practices which the conscientious, good companies will follow in the 21st century." He was right.

Since that time their progressive approach has only continued. More recently, they have established programs around sustainable design by making their design playbook open access,[31] and speaking out publicly against social inequality, standing by quarterback Colin Kaepernick as he brought more attention to the Black Lives Matter movement beginning in 2019. This is not to say that, since the soccer-ball scandal, they have an unblemished record, but they have shifted their corporate policies and practices to consistently lead in the execution and expansion of CSR initiatives within their own supply chain and the industry at large.

In addition to leading the global conversation on ethical practices, Nike has demonstrated that, counter to Milton Friedman's philosophy, increased corporate social responsibility can fuel business growth. Between 1996 and 2020, the company's valuation increased from $9 billion to $44 billion.[32] Is this solely a result of CSR? Of course not. But it is certainly reflective of the fact that CSR is now embedded within the operations, business plan, and consumer marketing of the firm. By laying out a clear strategy and creating the proper implementation channels, Nike has been able to both proactively address supply chain issues as they develop and leverage responsible sourcing as a business differentiator in an increasingly crowded market, bringing their skeptical consumers with them on the journey. Brands still need to compete on price, and Nike perhaps had a leg up on incorporating CSR efforts internally as it was already a dominant player in the market, but there are absolutely lessons that can be learned here by brands both large and small. There are ever-increasing consumer and shareholder expectations regarding corporate responsibility, and it is crucial for a corporation to have adequate controls and assurances when it comes to its increasingly distributed global supply chain. Missteps will continue to happen, and issues will arise as brands are able to look behind more curtains, but it is a brand's ability to be proactive and address negative impacts, as well as the factors that led to the issues in the first place, that dictate whether the brand can survive the crisis.

The Role of the Consumer

Equally, the Nike soccer balls incident demonstrates the increasing power of the consumer within the market. This concept of consumer control is a primary motivating factor for corporate behavior today and one that only grows stronger with increased access to information and social media as a communication channel. Consumer reaction is the primary reason that the brand team was with me in the Philippines, as well as why Nest has established so many powerful partnerships across a myriad of industries. People work for, and buy from, brands that they feel have an overall positive impact on society. And, just as it is important to consider history and how it has brought us to modern-day thinking on responsibility, it is crucial to think through all the competing interests at play within the supply chain, from consumers and shareholders to the teams that are tasked with the hard work of bringing products to market. That is where we will turn our attention next.

3

The Power Pathway: External and Internal Pressures on Global Supply Chains

"Power . . . is not an end in itself, but is an instrument that must be used toward an end."
—Jeane Kirkpatrick, Former US Ambassador to the United Nations

IN THE LAST chapter, we discussed how both public sentiment and government regulation, combined with increased globalization, have pressured corporations to alter their attitude toward supply chain responsibility over time. While this information can help you appreciate these issues from a macro level, you will also need to understand the pressures and politics of the *tactical* level if you want to play a more direct role in improving your company's sourcing practices or gauge the activities of a brand you shop from or invest in. *How do corporations make decisions that wind up impacting basket weavers like Laurie? What conversations take place thousands of miles away from her? What motivates and incentivizes the people having those conversations?*

There are plenty of books that focus on operational efficiencies—bottlenecks within a factory's production system and optimizing throughputs, for example—but this book will approach these topics differently. We will examine the pressures placed on decision-makers within the supply chain that can either encourage poor behavior or support transformative approaches. We will explore how some corporations create systemic change and greater visibility, accountability, and prosperity for the many actors involved in the creation and consumption of products. To do this we need to consider both external and internal power dynamics and acknowledge the different forces and incentives that influence decisions at all levels of an organization. We will start by looking at external forces—consumers and investors—and then work our way inwards, winding up back at Laurie's home in Pampanga.

Consumers

The Nike soccer ball incident is just one example of how increased consumer interest and expectations regarding corporate responsibility (and the accompanying change in consumer behavior) have made companies rethink their internal approaches. My first week in business school, one of my professors said something that radically shifted my thinking: *the consumer is the ultimate regulator of the market.*

This brought me back to our work at Nest (I attended business school while working at the organization). As we were designing our regulatory framework and compliance program for artisanal work, we did so in the hope that a universal standard would help home-based workers and raise their standards of living. But at the same time, we started hearing from large brands who were specifically asking us for help gaining transparency into their supply chains. Consumers, it turned out, were demanding to know where their products came from, and brands were responding to the pressure with very few places to turn. We were taken aback when brands that previously had zero presence in the artisan or handcraft sector approached us for partnership. At that moment I knew that within five years our sector, and Nest's work in particular, was going to change dramatically. We were uncovering a new truth: that many factories outsource labor to home-based workers—not just artisanal or craft work. This could include things such as sewing pom poms onto winter hats, or stringing seed bead jewelry, or even putting finished products into poly bags for shipping. It was an eye-opening moment for me. The brands knocking on our door were some of the largest in the world—companies that have enough in revenue to invest in strategic staff to focus on where the market is heading. In our case, it meant customers were taking a genuine interest in where and how their craft products were being produced. They wanted to know they were making a difference with their purchases by supporting a social good in some way. The need for visibility and responsible sourcing was about to enter the mainstream and was heading deeper into the supply chain than solely the factory.

As technology has advanced, the prevalence of widely available and rapidly shared information has had a massive impact on consumer behavior. Keep in mind that Facebook launched in 2004, and that between the year 2000 and 2016, global Internet users increased from 413 million to more than 3.4 billion.[1] Simultaneously, the 24-hour news cycle has dramatically increased awareness of global issues, but also the need for more "buzzy" news stories (i.e. scandals) to keep eyeballs glued to screens. By 2021, there were 75 channels listed explicitly as 24-hour news within the United States alone. How do you think executives feel about the ability for anyone, anywhere, at any time to take a picture of subpar working conditions or environmental damages from a factory with which their company is affiliated (however loosely) and post it to the Internet or share it with a national news outlet? What if a label with their company logo is visible on the factory floor of that subpar facility? Easier access to information, combined with a much larger megaphone, puts a lot more power into the hands of whistleblowers while creating new risks for companies.

As consumers consume (pun intended) this wealth of information, the rising purchasing power of both the millennial and Gen Z generations is having a huge market impact. This is where those futurists come in. Younger generations are willing to put more effort into researching products before buying them, and they're also willing to spend more if they believe their purchase will have a positive impact. A 2021 study showed that almost half of millennial customers surveyed (42%) would be willing to pay more for products that were sustainable.[2] To that end, work by New York University's Stern Center for Sustainable Business revealed that, between 2015 and 2019, products marketed as "sustainable" made up more than half the growth in consumer-packaged products (CPGs).[3] Not to be outdone, 90% of Gen Z consumers surveyed by Cone Communications believed that companies should actively help with environmental and social issues, with a whopping 75% of them doing their own research to make sure a company is actually doing what they say they are.[4] It's clear why so many huge brands were suddenly paying attention to their supply chain. If you want to stay in business, you need people to buy your products. What better way to differentiate yourself from competition by offering something that you know your customers are getting increasingly passionate about?

When Issues Arise

When a brand cares so deeply about pleasing its customers that it stretches the truth or overpromises on what it can realistically deliver, it puts the teams responsible for sourcing in a world of trouble. This often happens when the marketing and production (and corporate responsibility) teams are not actively communicating with one another. This is often called greenwashing, which we will explore in more detail in Chapter 8. For example, a brand creates beautiful new advertisements showcasing sustainability or environmentally friendly production without fully consulting the other departments to ensure that what they claim is true and/or happening. Or the claims become so aspirational that they no longer reflect the current reality of the company's operations. Alternately, issues arise if the customer gets confused by too many competing claims or labels. This is a natural phenomenon. With so many elements to consider within production (well-being of workers, raw-material sourcing, and environmental impact), a brand may want to communicate all its various commitments to a customer. While well-meaning, the assurances provided to the customer are only as good as the customer's understanding of them; that way, they can act based on their own value set through the purchase of that brand's products.

When the System Works

The brands that are most successful in activating their consumers—recognizable names such as Patagonia, Seventh Generation, and Allbirds—do so by both educating and listening to their customers. They are honest about how their values as a company translate to their decisions around product development and production, often going above and beyond to report back to their customer the impacts of their supply chains and their products. They keep the messaging clear and simple. They also focus on data, working with third-party partners to help verify their claims and back up their marketing with data to avoid risks of greenwashing or inaccurate storytelling. While they might tell multiple stories around human and environmental impact, they do so with consistency and clarity. They build extremely loyal followings, resulting in strong market positioning and defense against competition.

Investors

Just as consumer interest has risen around corporate behavior, so has investor interest. Even though an investor's primary goal is to make money (as Friedman laid out for us), many are starting to realize that a myopic focus on short-term profit can lead to long-term losses—some potentially catastrophic for the company, for people, or for the planet as a whole. For the past couple of decades, this has inspired a new class of investors to try and figure out ways to assess a company's commitment to and impact on sustainability. These are referred to as impact investors.

First coined in a 2005 study organized by the United Nations Environment Programme Initiative aptly titled, "Who Cares, Wins,"[5] the concept of Environmental, Social, and Governance (ESG) was conceived as a way to help these investors consider results beyond their bottom lines when deciding where to put their dollars. The term is a nod to the "triple-bottom-line" theory of returns, first introduced by John Elkington in 1994,[6] which assesses a firm based on their social and environmental impact as well as whatever monetary returns they gain. *Can you actually do well by doing good?* Yet, while the movement toward ESG metrics has gained momentum, it is still a subject of debate. As outlined in the McKinsey article, "Does ESG Really Matter—and Why?,"[7] one of the primary arguments against ESG ratings is that they too often end up as little more than a public relations distraction from actual business performance. According to this argument, it is too difficult to make actual impact, and no one is properly measuring it anyway, so why bother? And if and when impact is measured, it is not linked directly to financial performance (the company doing better financially as a result of its societal impact), it becomes less valuable data from a business perspective. On the other side of the argument, proponents of ESG focus on the fact that negative externalities are increasing—as exemplified by climate change and environmental degradation—and, as such, companies have an increased responsibility to build systems to measure impacts both positive and negative. In addition, some companies that have focused on ESG, such as Patagonia or Natura &Co., have done incredibly well financially, thereby proving that success is possible. Meanwhile, measurement is improving, and regulation is forcing more attention to be paid in this space, so ESG proponents will likely persevere.

Yet, the critics are not entirely wrong. A warning sign that the business community needed to provide some guardrails around use of the term "ESG" started in 1997. That year the oil company Shell issued its first sustainability report, which demonstrated how Shell was performing well in meeting their triple-bottom-line objectives. If an oil company can claim they are doing well from an ESG perspective, are there any teeth to the metrics? There has indeed been a lot of confusion related to investor reporting around these issues, and as Shell demonstrated, virtually any business could claim to be operating within an ESG framework if they are creative enough. There were too many different reporting mechanisms, which either looked at different impact data or presented findings in different ways—essentially with full discretion falling to the company to self-report their findings and impact from a wide variety of different partners. There was the Sustainability Accounting Standards Board (SASB), Climate Disclosures Standards Board (CDSB), International Integrated Reporting Council (IIRC), and Global Reporting Initiative (GRI), to name just a few. Fortunately, these reporting mechanisms have been rapidly consolidating in order to level the playing field and establish a more universal standard. In 2021, SASB and IIRC merged into a new Value Reporting Foundation, and the newly formed organization is working closely with GRI to achieve interoperability between the two standards. Where there were once multiple ways to report out, there will soon be only a handful of accepted metrics and frameworks, thereby creating consistency and further transparency in corporate reporting. This is good news for those who support ESG efforts, as, in the words often attributed to management theorist Peter Drucker, "You can only manage what you measure."

As corporate reporting becomes more standardized, investor eyes are starting to gaze beyond the CEOs and their firm-wide goals and upon the teams responsible for putting plans into action. In 2020, Larry Fink, CEO of the world's largest investment firm, Blackrock, wrote a letter to the CEOs of businesses that Blackrock had invested in stating, "Given the groundwork we have already laid engaging on disclosure, and the growing investment risks surrounding sustainability, we will be increasingly disposed to vote against management and board directors when companies are not making sufficient progress on sustainability-related disclosures and the business practices and plans underlying them."[8] Essentially, he was putting the market on notice that they better put up or shut up. No longer would Blackrock's investors be swayed by glossy marketing claims. Now they want to see real action taking place, and a commonality in reporting would help them do just that. Sounds a lot like those Gen Z and millennial consumers, right? To be clear, Blackrock is absolutely, positively about making money above all else. What other purpose, as Friedman would argue, does an investment company serve? But Fink, unlike Friedman, realizes that stakeholder capitalism is not about being "woke"; it's about ensuring longer-term profitability by incentivizing corporations to invest in their futures.

When Issues Arise

Activist investors with a Friedman-esque focus on profits can handcuff a firm's executive leadership team by voting against new ESG initiatives or even ousting the leadership in response to proposed changes. This can severely limit the amount of change within any given firm. Investors can also divest from businesses they feel are spending too much time focused on impact and sustainability, thereby reducing the amount of capital that is flowing to those same firms. As I am writing this, the State of Louisiana has declared that, to protect the fossil fuel industry, they will no longer be investing almost $800 million of state funds through Blackrock.[9]

When the System Works

The incorporation of responsible sourcing and sustainable business practices requires patient capital. This means that brands need investors to not punish them by selling off assets if the business is making new investments into innovation, infrastructure, or technologies that aim to reduce negative externalities in the future. Traditionally, a business is expected to report its financial performance to its investors every quarter, which leads to a short-term view on overall business performance. However as we will explore in Chapter 7, creative leaders, alongside open-minded investors, are creating solutions. Under CEO Paul Polman, when Unilever started leaning heavily into sustainability across its enormous number of brands, Polman announced they would no longer be providing quarterly reports beyond what was required from regulators. This gave the firm the space it needed to create systemic change and made sure the investors who stuck with them would be patient as they worked to build new systems. It paid off enormously. Today, 13 years after the initiative started, Unilever is considered one of the most successful examples of a brand turnaround when it comes to sustainable business practices.

The C-Suite and the Board

Given the demands of both consumers and investors, it is no wonder many C-suite leaders have put corporate responsibility—and responsible sourcing in particular—top of mind. The pressure for increased disclosures has led to widespread investor reporting around ESG metrics, but also to more attention on the relationship between environmental impacts and financial performance. For example, in 2010, the shoe company Puma published an Environmental Profit & Loss statement,[10] a first of its kind. The statement, which was released to investors alongside their traditional financial reports, assigned a dollar value to the natural resources used, the greenhouse gases emitted, and the overall carbon footprint of their supply chain. In total, the report valued the impacts at $133.5 million that year alone. The impact of Puma's Environmental P&L was powerful for the firm: as Stefan Seidel, head of corporate sustainability for Puma, stated, "One of the benefits of tagging impact factors with price is comparability . . . otherwise you could not tell which one is more important."[11] It led to Puma decreasing environmental impacts by 15% between 2011 and 2013. In 2015, fashion brand Stella McCartney adopted this practice, which has since spread across multiple sectors. Advocates say it helps create an internal culture of sustainable thinking and demonstrates both where the company is doing well and where there is room for improvement. Other corporations I've spoken to are currently hard at work developing social impact P&Ls, which will sit alongside their financial statements and environmental P&Ls. This work is just beginning, and it will be fascinating to see the results, what gets measured and reported, and who publishes first.

In addition to increased investor reporting, we are also seeing more executives issue firm-wide declarations of environmental and social impact goals. These have less to do with financial accounting and more to do with setting the tone and strategy of the overall business. Several factors could be driving this change. First, there's the United Nations Sustainable Development Goals (SDGs), a set of 17 goals put forward as a part of the 2030 Agenda for Sustainable Development, which was adopted by all UN Member States in 2015. The SDGs include aims to end poverty and hunger, promote sustained and equitable economic growth, and ensure access to sustainable energy for all. A body of the United Nations has been working closely with corporations to use this model within their own businesses by adopting goals that map to the UN's SDGs.

Another factor could be industry collaborations, such as the Climate Pledge to be Net Zero Carbon by 2040.[12] This cross-sector initiative brings together over 400 partners across 35 countries and uses shared metrics so that reporting can be aggregated to show collaborative—and thus, much larger—impact. The rise in internal reporting is also likely a reaction to consumer, investor, and employee calls for brands to pay more attention to the positive and negative impacts of their actions—and to quantify them.

Regardless of where the pressure is coming from, it's clear that stakeholders are looking toward the C-suite to set direction. A study published in April 2022 demonstrated that over half of employees (56%) would not consider a role at a company if they did not agree with its values.[13] Gen Z takes this even further, with 68% stating they would even be willing to take a 5% pay cut to work for a company with better values.

When the C-suite plays an active role, it tends to create a virtuous cycle: a sustainability and impact vision set by the C-suite means that the teams leading responsibility have a seat at the table and a recognized voice when it comes to business-related decisions. This, in turn, leads to reduced internal friction around impact-related decisions, leading to greater impact overall. When such a directive is backed by financial incentive structures (bonuses) that reward employees based on overall firm success metrics rather than individual or departmental metrics, it further facilitates collaboration. At Nest, we have seen this firsthand: when the CEO creates an action plan around impact, all parties work to figure out how to row in the same direction. A recent example of the C-suite leading the effort took place in 2019, when Laura Alber, president and CEO of the Williams-Sonoma, Inc. family of brands, announced a partnership with Nest and Fairtrade USA as part of the firm's commitment to having 75% of its products meet one or more of their social and environmental initiatives by 2030.[14]

Beyond pressure from consumers, investors, and employees, the C-suite has also become more engaged in CSR due to increased government regulation. In the past few years, we've seen an increase in new policy around supply chains that have forced even the most skeptical CSR adopters to pay attention. These efforts started in Europe (as most progressive business ideas do) when, in 2017, France passed the Corporate Duty of Vigilance Act. In 2021,

Germany followed suit by passing the Supply Chain Due Diligence Act. These triggered the European Union to contemplate its own EU-wide measures, all of which would be designed to hold a company *legally* responsible for any human-rights or environmental abuses that take place anywhere within their supply chains. These laws would also impact any non-European businesses that do a certain amount of business on the continent. Remember how Nike initially shirked responsibility, claiming that the issues of child labor were not really their problem since they were happening in contracted facilities? These laws force companies to accept accountability.

Meanwhile, in the United States, tensions with China have jump-started some supply chain initiatives of their own. American officials have expressed particular concern about the growing evidence that China is using forced labor among the Uyghur population in the Xinjiang Province. This region is responsible for about 90% of China's cotton exports, the equivalent of roughly 20% of global cotton production, and thus has far-reaching impacts for garment manufacturing. To combat the concern, the US government passed legislation in September 2020 to prohibit the import of any products that were created using the forced labor of Uyghurs. To enforce this, Congress has empowered US Customs and Border Protection agents to seize any goods from the Xinjiang region unless the importing brand can demonstrate they were made without forced labor. This is a massive shift in corporate responsibility regulation and, while an isolated case, shows how much power the government has to influence corporate action.

When Issues Arise

While it is tempting for brands to make public declarations in an effort to boost their recognition and consumer confidence, doing so can be dangerous if those declarations are not followed up with a concerted strategy around implementation. Employees need to clearly understand the role they are intended to play in the initiative; otherwise, it will most certainly fall flat. In addition, if the C-suite makes promises that run counter to the brand's history or expressed values, the effort will be called into question both internally and externally. Equally as dangerous, if a brand is saying one thing but doing the opposite, its actions, once exposed, will be considered greenwashing and cause even more reputational damage.

When the System Works

The C-suite and board are able to create positive change when they not only state their bold intentions publicly and internally, but when they help create the road map the firm can take to reach those goals. They facilitate the creation of teams, and potentially leadership positions, to create the tactics needed for forward momentum. They embrace the creation of measurable goals in order for the company to ascertain how they are doing on meeting their objectives. And they create a culture of innovation and collaboration, where employees at all levels can break a few eggs in pursuit of the goal without fearing retribution. Paul Polman, the former CEO of Unilever, whom we discussed earlier in this chapter, represents a real-world example of this type of leadership. When the commitment to sustainability comes from the top, all teams are empowered to transform lofty goals into practical ambitions.

Internal Operations

If the C-suite provides the direction, what happens next? Continuing our journey of the baskets made by Laurie, let's walk through the various teams and corporate politics at play in turning sustainability goals into a reality. Please remember that this example could easily be translated across many other industries, including fashion, consumer-packaged goods, mechanical manufacturing, food, and many more—even if it may look different in some of those applications.

The Design Team

The creative design team provides the aesthetic direction of a brand with the focus on consumer trends. They work in mood boards and sketches and are steeped in artistry. It is here that a product's journey starts. The creative design team envisions what an ideal product might look like—how it builds off consumer trends but differentiates itself for the brand. They start with sketches followed by sampling and prototyping, until they possess a mock-up that feels right. These creatives work hand in hand with the technical design team, who help to create the "instructions" for how the producers can replicate the envisioned design. The end result is a "tech pack" for producers—the schematics regarding precisely how an item is to look, its exact dimensions, and often also supplying an approved sample. While the creative team's outputs are artistic, those of the technical design team are more scientific.

When Issues Arise

If not careful, it can be easy for the design teams to operate in a bubble without considering the ripple effect their actions have on the later stages of production. For example, they may fail to consider how last-minute design changes can wreak havoc on timelines or how certain production techniques require environmentally harmful materials or processes that run counter to their firm's ESG commitments. Too often, design teams can forget to think about the many other human hands involved in actually making the products they've only conceived of, and that their choices have impacts.

When the System Works

I have seen design teams establish true relationships with their producers and their capabilities, enabling them to work together to establish
entirely new ways of creating a product or developing a new design. One
Nest Advisory Board member, who works in the fashion industry, insists
that each new member of her team spend time on the factory floor, trying their hand at actually making the products they will be designing.
Instead of just letting them sketch out beautiful clothing ideas, she has
them sit down and try to sew them. They are not expected to make
something perfectly of course, but they are expected to walk away with
a new respect for the skills required in production and to remember the
men and women at the end of the supply chain every time they work on
a new collection. Now every time I travel with brand teams, I insist they
sit with the craft workers we meet and do the same. Go ahead. Try to
make that basket you are so familiar with. Not so easy, is it? While this
exercise is perhaps not practical for all large multinational companies,
there are ways to replicate this effort through education, in-person or
virtual meetings, and ensuring creative teams understand their role in
corporate commitments around social responsibility.

Production/Sourcing

This team tends to "own" the supplier relationships. They interface
with the producer businesses on a regular basis and get real-time
feedback on orders and production status. If something goes wrong,
they serve as the facilitator between the brand and its vendors.
They see to it that producers can successfully deliver the products
conceived by the design team.

When Issues Arise

Sourcing can be an extremely high-pressure job, particularly if the
team's primary goal (i.e. the metric used to assess their performance
and determine bonuses) is to deliver on time and under budget so

the company can make money. With supply chain complexities worsening from extreme weather to global pandemics, this role often has to deal with significant stressors. Due to this stress, the people in this position can find themselves in situations where they feel like the "bad cop." When not properly trained, this can lead to unhealthy and unsustainable environments and cultures. For example, I have witnessed production teams verbally abuse producers when things are not going well. Not only is this way of working unsustainable for the production team, but it is suboptimal for the production partners. If the producer fears they'll lose an account if they can't meet—or even exceed—expectations, they may be tempted to cut corners. They may reduce spending on safety and compliance efforts, under-pay their workers or refuse to pay them overtime, or force workers to work long hours that compromise their health and well-being. They may also embark on unauthorized subcontracting in order to keep up production numbers. In addition, this profit-first, high-pressure approach tends to encourage the production team to bounce from one producer to another, or one country to another, in a never-ending quest to secure the lowest price. As a result, these brands fail to build relationships, trust, or insight into their full supply chain.

When the System Works

While it can be stressful when things go wrong, this role can provide an opportunity to be a true changemaker when things go right. With stronger and more long-term supplier relationships, producers start to be more open and honest when issues arise and can work hand-in-hand with the production team to address systemic challenges. For example, in one case, I had a producer talk to a brand about the fact that last-minute increases in order size meant that the producer was being forced to outsource production to subcontractors that had not yet been authorized. They did not want to do this, but they felt limited in their options to meet brand needs. Trust allowed for transparency and mutual problem solving. By working *with* the producers instead of in conflict with them, the brand was able to start planning a little further in advance so as to give the producer a longer runway. At the same time, the producer began onboarding additional contractors into the Nest Ethical Handcraft compliance program in case they needed them in the future. A win-win for everyone. This is also an example of how the production team can act as the eyes and ears for the company, bringing the challenges they encounter back to the other teams so that they can work to address them together.

The Merchandizing Team

I believe merchandizers are the lynchpins of any initiative to improve sourcing practices. For any CSR effort to succeed, there needs to be a business case for it. The merchandizing team focuses on profit margin across product offerings, which means they are responsible for many of the business-related decisions regarding a collection. They crunch numbers from a historical sales performance perspective, and they organize each year's (or season's) offering to meet a specific revenue target. As a merchandizer your biggest nightmares are: (1) a collection that misses your revenue targets or, worse, loses money and (2) an absence or shortage of the right products on the shelf. The latter could result from a late or incomplete shipment or a higher than predicted demand for a particular product.

When Issues Arise

If the merchandizing team is solely focused on margin, they can act as roadblocks for those trying to address systemic issues. For example, they may be unwilling to increase prices to meet minimum or living-wage goals because they believe their customers will balk at paying more and they are incentivized to keep profit margins consistent. Sometimes, an increase of less than a dollar per product will mean the workers at the farthest ends of the supply chain—workers like Laurie—start making fairer wages.

When the System Works

If merchants are active members of a cross-functional team and understand how the brand hopes to create positive impact, they can apply a business lens to the conversation and help meet those goals. They can merchandize a collection to ensure that overall profit margin is within target, even if they sacrifice some profit in exchange for achieving sustainability goals. In addition, when the merchandizing team is included in CSR conversations, they can encourage longer-term sourcing relationships by not putting undue pressure on production to chase the lowest price. This is another reason why it is important for these commitments to come from the top; merchandizers need permission to focus on dual goals: profit margins *and* social responsibility.

Responsible Sourcing/CSR

This team is on the front line of systems change within a firm. They are the guardians of corporate reputation and the eyes and ears paying attention to the behavior and trustworthiness of producer partners. Ideally, this team is also tasked with educating other teams within the company on best practices and setting impact metrics that each team can track. As laid out in Ernst and Young's publication, created in partnership with the UN Global Compact, "The State of Sustainable Supply Chains,"[15] there are essentially three ways these teams can work within a corporation: siloed, hybrid, or integrated.

The *siloed* model consists of a group of advocates that are isolated from other company teams. This breeds stereotypes that they are the "hippies in Birkenstocks" that shout at the rain, every now and then publishing thought pieces on the ways in which a company should incorporate impact and sustainability. The challenge with this model is that the advocates' work has no direct link to the firm's business decisions, and trust is rarely built internally, leaving their counsel to be seen as advice rather than a directive or strategy.

The *hybrid* model increases the engagement of the responsible sourcing team by providing them a seat at the table for strategy conversations. Still, they remain somewhat of an afterthought. Business decisions get made, and then this team comes in to see if there are ways to improve their sustainability. They can work to establish processes that they hope other teams follow, but they are not factored directly into operating decisions.

The *integrated* model is the gold standard. Under this model, all decisions begin with a focus on sustainability and social impact. Each business decision must pass through this lens before it is implemented, giving it equal weight alongside price and product viability. In an integrated model, the CSR team actively trains other departments in best practices. To be clear, this is the ideal state. It is also where first-mover brands establish best practices around sustainability, thereby creating a model for others to follow while differentiating themselves from competitors.

Other Teams

There are certainly many more hands involved in the process of getting a product to shelf than those called out above. Quality assurance/testing teams make sure products meet their expected specifications, performing onsite quality checks, as well as reviewing safety tests for things such as flammability and toxicity. Finance approves the upfront deposits on products (which is critical in the

Nest handcraft sector, where businesses may not have the working capital they need to pay for raw materials or worker wages up front). This team sets the payment terms, which are often 90 or 120 days after the products have been received. The logistics team can help create efficiencies within the shipment of products, particularly with regard to carbon footprint. They also help create packing materials, so if you want to use fully recycled/recyclable packing materials, this is the team to talk to.

Corporations are complex organisms. When this is understood and built into corporate social responsibility efforts, teams can collaborate, creating a greater likelihood of success. When the interests of sustainability are siloed or do not have leadership support, the efforts will be fragmented. Design and ultimate execution require careful planning and cross-team training and integration.

The Role of Incentives

In a traditional business model, each team receives bonuses for the value their team brings to the table. For example, the sourcing or production teams will receive financial incentives if they can deliver product on time and at or under budget. Merchandizers receive bonuses related to the amount of profit they bring to the company. When your performance in these areas directly impacts how much money you make, you tend to focus your attention on those aspects of your job. When this happens, incentives can actually be counterproductive to firm-wide goals, especially regarding sustainability.

In an ideal scenario, everyone in the firm would receive bonuses equally, based on overall business performance, and/or any incentive model would factor in sustainability targets. Taking Larry Fink's argument to the next level, if a CEO declares that impact and sustainability are important and matter to the consumer, all teams could be incentivized to work toward those commitments. If the consumer then demonstrates that, indeed, these values matter by spending more with your brand, overall business profits will meet or exceed expectations and all team members benefit. The beauty of this approach is that it reduces any friction between teams and gets everyone to focus on the overarching objectives. One example of this approach was taken by Mastercard in 2022. Instead of simply looking at the company's financial performance when calculating employee bonuses for the year, the company now factors in environmental and social-impact metrics as well.[16] This will surely incentivize team members to focus less on profit exclusively and work harder to achieve CSR objectives. A very bold step, to be sure!

The Role of Producers

While internal corporate teams are critical to advancing responsible sourcing, we must also consider the role of producers—the factories, vendors, and individuals who make the goods consumers buy. Just as we saw with the Nike example, most brands today do not produce the goods they sell. Instead, they rely on third parties to create products for them. As if the world of internal corporate politics wasn't complex enough, just wait until you consider the vast network of connections within the production system—and the various pressures acting upon it.

Corporations often hold significant power in their relationships with factory owners since they determine who ultimately receives their business. There are thousands of factories worldwide who are constantly competing for brand attention based on price, quality, capacity, reliability, and ability to scale. Even after they land an order, factories must often adapt to the shifting needs of the brand partner as the types and/or quantities of products they order change. Factories may need to factor in operating costs for specialized production techniques (for example, a particular type of beadwork, embroidery, or other embellishment on a garment or household good). They may need to manage the ups and downs of order volume or the fast-follow orders that may come for products that exceed sales expectations. Additionally, many factories must create models that seasonally produce items such as holiday decorations, winter hats, or bathing suits, which don't require full-time workers or supply chains that operate throughout the year. All these challenges may lead a factory to incorporate subcontracted production, a layer further away from the eyes of the brand (not to mention the consumer).

Additionally, factories themselves need to partner with vendors who supply the raw materials or basic goods that the factory then finishes according to the brand partner's specifications. As a result, a brand's supply chain is typically broken out into tiers of production. Depending on the type of product, the tiers may vary slightly. For illustration purposes, let's use garments as an example. Consider the tiers of production involved in the production of a cotton t-shirt.

> Tier 1: Finishing. This is where the shirt actually gets sewn together and where it gets packaged for shipment. This is often the primary business a brand engages with directly. Until recently, it was also the only tier that most brands considered from a social and environmental impact perspective.
>
> Tier 2: Processing. This is where the fabric gets woven, dyed, and perhaps embellished.
>
> Tier 3: Raw-material processing. This is where the thread used to make the fabric is spun and dyed.
>
> Tier 4: Raw-material harvesting. This is the farm (or in reality the hundreds of different farms) where the cotton for the thread is produced.

As you look at this preceding list, think about the increasing complexity and numbers of people involved the further you go down the supply chain. For example, what if a raw material processor buys their cotton from a wholesaler instead of directly from the farmer? How could you possibly trace the actual farmer in that scenario? How can you guarantee that it is organic or responsibly farmed?

Also consider—as we saw in Laurie's example—that not everything is produced in a factory. Chocolate, coffee, minerals, precious metals, and yes, the handcrafted goods of Nest's world all start their journey far outside the organized structure of a four-walled facility with its rules, regulations, and protocols. No chocolate bars could exist without the work of independent (aka small-holder) farmers in countries such as the Ivory Coast, Ghana, or Ecuador, many of whom work at the edge of the jungle with little to no transparency into their conditions. The palm oils used in nearly 70% of the world's food and cosmetic products rely on farmers in places such as Madagascar, who feel the pressures of clear-cutting rainforest and eliminating valuable environmental landscapes in order to drive the economic machine and global demands for their commodity. And handmade products such as Laurie's basket rely on a workforce of more than 300 million people from within their homes or informal community workshops before they arrive on the shelves of big-box and high-end retailers alike. Historically it has been this last mile of production that has always been overlooked due to the complexity of the supply chain. Thankfully, that is changing thanks to globally recognized standards such as Nest's Seal of Ethical Handcraft and FairTrade USA, or the work of cutting-edge businesses such as chocolate bar manufacturer Tony's Chocolonely with its tracking and reporting of child labor in its supply chain, or shoemaker Nisolo with its reporting of how it is working toward living wages for every worker in their factories. The rise of blockchain technology has also enabled increased transparency into the many tiers of production.

How to Address the Complexity of Global Sourcing

Given this complexity, how can a brand, which may be sourcing products from 20 or more countries, increase its visibility into its supply chain and better monitor their social and environmental impact? One way is through the utilization of standards, auditing, and certification systems. Let us explore that solution in the next chapter.

4

Pulling Back the Curtain: The Basics of Standard-Setting and Auditing to Increase Transparency

"The single most important ingredient in the recipe for success is transparency because transparency builds trust."

—Denise Morrison,
former President & CEO of the Campbell Soup Company

NOW THAT WE'VE introduced the various actors involved in getting product to market, let's focus our attention on one team in particular: responsible sourcing. How can one team have eyes and ears in multiple countries at once, especially if they have to deal with dozens, if not hundreds, of factories and producers in each? In this chapter, we will explore one of the key solutions to this problem: systems of standard-setting and the auditing processes that increase transparency throughout the supply chain. We will also look at how brands can communicate their commitment to this process to their customers through the use of certifications and product seals.

Who Is the Responsible Sourcing Team?

Responsible sourcing teams are typically composed of multiple individuals (or, in some cases, smaller teams) who manage different product categories or specialize in a specific area of compliance (e.g. environmental impacts, social impacts, or government regulations). In most cases, larger firms will have larger teams, but that is not always true. In fact, the size of the team can be a quick way to gauge a company's commitment and investment into their responsible practices. Responsible sourcing teams will often have representatives at both the headquarters level and within specific regions or countries where significant amounts of their production take place. These in-country teams help mitigate the risk involved with using contracted production instead of vertical integration. Because they work relatively close to the actual producers, these local teams have relatively easy access to the people actually making the brand's products and can establish stronger connections with them than those who work at a corporate headquarters oceans away. They can act as the face of the brand with the network of factories or producers and constantly reinforce brand expectations and vigilance. Locally based, they will have a stronger sense of the cultural norms as well as geopolitical dynamics at play in a given geography. For example, in-country teams will be able to alert the brand to growing political unrest that may disrupt supply chains, notify headquarters of changes in governmental regulation or labor law, as well as help uncover challenges that workers face beyond the factory floor. Examples may include hyperinflation, water-access issues, viral outbreaks, and natural disasters. In-country teams also often wear multiple hats. While they may be members of the corporate responsible sourcing team, they also work with the production teams to monitor ongoing production, coordinate sampling, and provide real-time updates regarding the status of various orders.

But when it comes specifically to *responsible* sourcing, how do these teams ascertain the performance of a production partner? With whom do they partner to perform those assessments? And how can they tell if a particular producer is acting in accordance with the brand's expectations even when they (or an auditing firm) are not in the room? In other words, against what ruler are they measuring performance? Without some sort of generally accepted framework, how can producers and sourcing teams be on the same page and ensure quality and compliance? This is where standards come in.

Standards: The Rule Book to Follow

As I referenced briefly back in Chapter 1, brands will often have their own codes of conduct that stipulate, at a high level, their expectations for production partners. Common themes include the prohibition of things generally regarded as unethical (e.g. forced or child labor, bribery, restricted or banned chemicals) as well as requirements that the producer comply with local laws and environmental regulations. These codes provide a bird's-eye view of responsible sourcing and signal to everyone (investors and consumers included) what values the brand seeks to uphold. You can generally find these codes of conduct online by searching the brand's name along with the phrase "supplier code of conduct."

The responsible sourcing team is able to take compliance to a much more granular level by adopting more rigorous guidelines, known as standards. These provide a benchmark by which a brand can measure how closely a production facility aligns with its code of conduct and values. Through the use of standards, brands also create the road map that allows them to test a specific producer for compliance. Each standard is then measured or assessed during the auditing process providing a factory or production partner with the rule book they will need to follow. You may already be familiar with the existence of these guidelines without realizing it: those consumer-facing labels such as Fair Trade, or B Corp, or LEED are each built upon a unique set of standards.

Standards are complex systems that require significant effort to create and then maintain. Creators must follow a set methodology for developing them in order for others in the industry to consider them as valid and adopt them. This is critical to ensure that they are fully comprehensive, map to and align with global norms or other similar standards that are already in use, align with global labor law standards, and are inclusive of the needs of wide-ranging corporations. It is also important that a myriad of stakeholders is considered: a brand should not follow standards set solely by the industry but also consider workers themselves, local stakeholders and service providers, and labor rights organizations. It is further complicated in that these global norms and laws change, so standards must be continually reviewed and revised. In fact, there is an entire organization called the International Social and Environmental Accreditation and Labelling (ISEAL) Alliance[1] that establishes best practices for setting and then maintaining standards. In my own experience, when Nest realized that no viable compliance system existed for the home-based and small-workshop production facilities we support, we decided to create our own, relying heavily on ISEAL resources and guidance to do so.

Most standards are created by nonprofit organizations (such as Nest) who are focused on specific issues tied to their mission. Most standards follow one of two foci: environmental or labor. Nonprofits, such as the Rainforest Alliance or LEED, are focused on environmental concerns and therefore create standards regarding the sustainable practices behind raw-material sourcing, production, or, in LEED's case, building design and construction. Others, such as Nest or Fair Trade USA, have missions that focus more on the treatment of workers in the supply chain and are therefore considered social or labor standards. Either way, it is important to note that these standards are not created, owned, or maintained by an individual brand but instead by an objective third-party organization, which is then further overseen by organizations such as ISEAL. These layers ensure that conflicts of interest and other potential risks are mitigated to the fullest extent possible.

Perhaps the best way to illustrate the process of standard creation and adoption is to walk through our experience at Nest.

Setting the Standard

Nest was founded in 2006 by my wife Rebecca (the writer of the Foreword of this book). She graduated with her master's degree in social work and initially envisioned Nest as a way to support globally based women's cooperatives. She harbored no ambition to create a compliance standard for artisan homeworkers. However, in

2014, our leadership team found ourselves considering how to do just that due to an ever-changing consumer environment where artisan-made products were scaling into mainstream retailers. Our mission has always been to build the capacity of artisans and makers in the United States and abroad, enabling them to more successfully utilize market forces to increase their impact and ensure economic equity for the women involved in craft production. However, as we worked with brands and advocated for the sourcing of handmade products, we were faced with a very real challenge: brands hesitated to source products from this supply chain, or to tell their consumers that they were sourcing from it, because there was too much risk. As we have discussed, artisans are laboring from their homes or informal workshops, not regulated factories. Further complicating the situation, artisans are paid per piece rather than a salary, and their work can be seasonal or vary substantially, making tracking records and payment even more complicated. It is also often made in the form of cash payments leading to significant transparency complications when it comes to worker pay. Time and time again we heard some version of the same refrain: *we love the look and feel of the product and know our customer would love it, too. But how can we put something on our shelves if we have no assurance that children were not involved in the process? Or that the people who produced it were paid fairly and working under safe conditions?* Taken together, this feedback triggered a huge light-bulb moment for us. We could provide all the business training and capacity-building programs in the world, and consumer trends could indicate a rapid rise in interest in artisan products, but if we were unable to bridge the gap between brand risk aversion and the market opportunity, what was the point? Without the market reach of larger brands and retailers, many artisan cooperatives would struggle with the scale necessary to provide the meaningful employment so necessary in their communities. So we set out to make this form of labor visible and safe in accordance with standards that were agreed upon across the retail industry but, most critically, while appreciating the cultural nuance of home-based labor.

The first thing we did, as per ISEAL recommendations, was to ensure that a new standard was going to be relevant by looking at the current landscape of compliance and assessing the need for a new program. We did this by performing a landscape analysis of 30+ standards and compliance systems that our industry partners used or highlighted as relevant. We found that not a single existing model assessed or monitored handcraft work in a way that was globally applicable while providing brands with the transparency they needed to make informed sourcing decisions. We found that the vast majority of existing standards focused only on factory production and may, at most, include a single question about the use of subcontractors or decentralized production models. The few standards that considered craft work were focused on a specific craft type (e.g. rugs) or a specific geography (e.g. within India). We also conducted a double-blind survey of multinational brands and confirmed that a large majority (92%) had artisans or homeworkers in their supply chain yet no viable way to approach responsible sourcing with this group. Finally, through surveying our rapidly growing stakeholder group of handcraft businesses, we learned that their past experiences with responsible sourcing teams made them feel like the teams were trying to fit a round peg in a square hole. Without an alternative solution, brand representatives approached these cottage industry supply chains of homes the same way they would a regulated, four-walled factory. For example, a sourcing-team member might check to see if there were fire exit signs inside a single-family house. Or, at an open-air workshop like Laurie's in the Philippines, they told makers they needed to clearly indicate evacuation routes. *Why would you need arrows pointing to a door when there are no walls surrounding half the structure?* Clearly, there was a huge gap between expectations and reality.

Next, again following ISEAL guidance, we sought to create a system that represented the desired outcomes of all the stakeholders involved. In order to do so, we established a Steering Committee that consisted of several stakeholders and experts: representatives from industry-leading brands including Eileen Fisher, Patagonia, Target, and Williams-Sonoma; experts in compliance and auditing from firms such as Bureau Veritas; other non-governmental organization (NGO) leaders from labor rights organizations such as The Centre for Child Rights and Business; and the leaders of handcraft businesses. This committee helped Nest craft a program that ensured it uniquely met the needs of very diverse partners. Creating alignment across all these points of view took considerable effort, and we had to make several difficult decisions along the way. For instance, early on we debated whether we should include significant environmental regulations within our standards. A few brands on the committee were extremely focused on sustainability as a key differentiator for their businesses, and the handcraft sector had little transparency into the environmental conditions in which production took place. In the end, we opted to focus first on the labor side of the equation. We were experts in craft-business operations, not the science behind environmental regulations and testing. We realized that trying to take on both standards at the same time right from the start would severely bog down our development process. While difficult, we had to make strategic decisions to ensure the standard met the needs of our partners but could be executed successfully after launch.

Using existing factory models as a starting point, we then spent two years drafting our Nest Ethical Compliance Standards for Homes and Small Workshops. It contained specific guidance on issues of worker rights and business transparency; child advocacy and protection; fair compensation and benefits; and health and safety, broken down into more than 100 individually measurable requirements. The next step was to open the proposed standard up for a period of public review and comment, which would ensure that we incorporated as many points of view and priorities into the standard as possible. Nest published the draft version online; announced the period of review via an email and press release to our entire network of artisan cooperatives, brands, and retailers; and aligned NGOs as well as countless other compliance organizations. We set up an email address to handle any feedback and suggestions and waited to hear what people had to say. This process, and the corresponding refinements, only served to strengthen the program, as we were indeed presented with additional ideas and contextual examples to consider. For example, one business leader pointed out that some of our proposed requirements made sense for small workshops but were not necessarily as clear for home-based labor. In our early drafts, we had added a provision that every production location should have access to a functioning smoke alarm, but many homes around the world lack electricity. We altered the standard to require that all workshops have smoke alarms, as well as any homes where dangerous processes or equipment are being utilized, but decided to forgo that requirement in a home where someone would be doing handwork that does not require or use equipment that could be a hazard, making it a just a recommendation in those circumstances. For added clarity we made sure to define what constituted a "dangerous" process or piece of equipment via a lengthier definition section in the standard.

In parallel with the public review process, we needed to pressure-test the application of these standards in real-world situations. We ran pilots of the program across five different countries and 42 sites, learning as we went. Not only were we able to identify weak points in our standard, but we were also able to formulate an appropriate methodology for how to assess a business's performance in relation to the standard. In a typical model, an audit directly maps quantitative data points to the standard itself, creating a scorecard for a facility.

In industry terms, this scorecard is called a corrective action plan (CAP) and is used by the responsible sourcing team to indicate whether a producer is compliant and where they require improvement. As with many systems, Nest's is a scaled scoring model. This means that the more severe an issue is, the more impact it has on the overall score. For example, a discovery of active child labor would produce a much more severe score than, say, the lack of a sign indicating that child labor is prohibited. Additionally, many standards, such as Nest's, require that there is dual verification for each standard, meaning that in the assessment process, the auditor has two methods to determine if the producer is compliant. For example, one could look at wage records to determine if the wages were provided and were at or above a required minimum wage, and then the auditor can also interview workers confirming the accuracy of the records. These processes help ensure the accuracy of the data being collected.

In addition to developing the assessment or auditing methodology, Nest identified ways in which our program actually needed to deviate from more traditional factory programs. In a traditional model, an audit is the first step in measuring compliance. If the audit reveals areas that need improvement, the factory is then expected to take the necessary steps to become compliant. However, in these scenarios, the production facilities already have established protocols that lay out the steps needed to address compliance issues. Factory compliance is not new, and most are under the rigorous oversight of multiple programs as well as government regulation already. Handcraft work, by contrast, takes place in the informal economy, with verbal contracts, cash payments, and a population with a high likelihood of illiteracy. These businesses often have no formal systems set up to address the compliance issues that are defined in labor standards. Without even the foundational processes in place, any business that scores low on our assessment would face potentially devastating consequences if a brand then chose not to partner with them. Given

Nest's commitment to supporting these workers, we realized we needed to rely on our capacity-building expertise to create a training-first approach toward implementing our standard. That way, we can work directly with these businesses to meet our standard helping build foundational knowledge of these systems within decentralized settings, ideally increasing the likelihood of ultimate success.

Once our review and piloting period had run their course, we were finally ready to officially launch the Nest Ethical Compliance Standards for Homes and Small Workshops. We unveiled the standard in 2017 in partnership with the United Nations Office of Partnership. The event was attended by brands, handcraft businesses, and industry leaders who signed their commitment to abide by this new program on stage at the UN. It was a fantastic achievement, but the real work had only just begun. To keep a standard system current, we needed a routine of reevaluation, public feedback, and adjustment at least every five years. Nest established a Standards Committee of outside experts to help us field any grievances related to the system and to help provide program updates on a regular basis. With such a nuanced and ever-changing supply chain, each new vendor that enrolls in our program provides a new perspective, as do the changing labor laws in the 27 countries where our program is now being used. We have been steadily incorporating this experience into the work. New health and safety standards, new approaches to child labor remediation, and new wage setting requirements are just a few of the ways we have strengthened the program over time.

Auditing

Congratulations! You have set and launched a standard of compliance, or more likely several standards, for your supply chain. Now how are you going to monitor it? While it might seem easiest to send these standards to your production partners and ask for them to self-evaluate, that can, of course, be complicated and lead to inaccurate or overstated reporting. It also might be tempting to have your team travel to the field and assess your partners yourselves—that way, you are the eyes and ears and see the situation firsthand. Unfortunately, this, too, is problematic as it leads to potential conflicts of interest. It might be hard to remain objective if a brand really wants to source product from a specific vendor, and a vendor is less likely to be honest with a brand partner about compliance issues when a potential business deal is on the line. Enter the rise of the auditing sector.

While nonprofits often establish and own compliance standards, auditing firms (who often operate for profit) typically perform facilities assessments to those approved standards.* There are a few reasons for this separation between standard-setting and auditing. Firstly, standard-setting organizations tend to focus on education and remediation with businesses, helping them improve their systems to meet the demands of the standard. As such, they have expertise in training as opposed to assessing. In addition, there can be financial incentive for the standard-setting body to report that a producer is compliant: if they meet certain criteria, the producer can be certified and, in exchange, the standard-setting body may receive a licensing fee for that certification mark. An independent auditing firm can help provide objectivity as well as a specialized skill set. While standard-setting bodies are focused on educating businesses on their standard and best practices, auditing firms focus on the data collection and verification systems, and its members are typically experts on a number of different standard systems. In order to maintain impartiality, audit firms will rotate the auditors that visit a specific factory each year. To take objectivity even a step further, brands will often rotate the auditing firms they use for

---

* To clarify, when I refer to auditors and the auditing process within this chapter, I am not referring to a fiscal audit but rather the measurement of how a producer is performing related to a specific standard.

auditing work every few years as well. The audit firms are generally engaged (and paid) by facilities that are interested in demonstrating their compliance with standards due to brand requirements, industry norms, or as a way to differentiate themselves from their competitors. The brand will stipulate to a production facility which standards or certifications it accepts and will often dictate which auditing firms can be engaged for the verification, but the producer is the one that pays for the firm to assess their facility. To ensure that the firm can assess a standard properly, the standard-setting body will offer accreditation for auditors who want to learn that specific system. To be accredited, the auditor will need to attend ongoing courses and trainings and demonstrate an understanding of the standard and the methodology used to perform the audit. The standard-setting body may review their work and reports, and the audited facilities may be surveyed on their experiences with particular auditors to maintain quality control regarding their standard.

When it comes time for an on-site assessment, the auditors inform the producer they will arrive within a wide period of time (e.g. three to four weeks) so that the facility does not have the opportunity to hide any risk areas or manipulate records and systems to try and deceive the auditor. During the course of their visit to the site, the auditor will review records, speak with management, conduct private and confidential interviews with randomly selected workers, and tour the facility itself. Each observation and piece of information gathered will inform the scoring on the CAP and provide recommended remediation steps to correct issues. This all used to be done via a simple clipboard, but with the advancements of technology, they are often done on tablets, with the capability of providing photographic evidence of the issues found and instantly uploading findings. A factory audit normally takes between one and two days (depending on the size of the facility and the complexity of the audit). The generated CAP is first shared with the facility, giving them an opportunity to express their disagreement with any of the findings or to add any additional context that might be helpful. The finalized CAP is then shared with the facility, as well as with any of the brands that are sourcing products from that factory. As I indicated earlier, if the business performs well, it can often receive a certification mark or seal, which can be used internally to help with risk mitigation or in external marketing to entice consumers who want to support brands aligned with that specific standard. Some of the most popular consumer-facing certifications are Fair Trade,* B Corp, and the Leaping Bunny cruelty-free seal, among many others.

It is important to note that there are times when a standard-setting body chooses not to utilize auditing firms to perform the assessments; the Nest system currently operates this way. We initially planned to set up a standard operating model, with Nest owning the standard and auditors performing assessments. However, as we worked with our Steering Committee and partners (brands and handcraft producers alike), we learned they wanted Nest to remain more deeply connected in the compliance process since we were the experts in the landscape and had a much better understanding of the context than a more traditional audit firm who, for years, have been solely focused on factory environments. The nuance of being in a home is not simply one of size, it is also cultural: how an auditor shows up to a provided dwelling is very important to ensuring trust and well-being of that artisan participant. We realized that, at least in the beginning, it would take much too long for auditors to get trained on this part of the supply chain and our more nuanced methodology rooted in social work. The building of an accreditation model for auditing

---

* There are actually multiple Fair Trade organizations, each with their own standard. Some of these standards are more robust than others. For example, Fair Trade USA has been widely held as a strong compliance system, having started in agriculture and expanded into factory production. On the opposite extreme, there are some Fair Trade organizations that amount to more of a membership organization versus an audited standard, but they still have a consumer-facing mark or seal.

firms would have massively delayed the ability to get transparency into the sector. In situations like ours, then, it became critical that we create additional steps to maintain impartiality. We do this by using different Nest team members to perform the training work versus the assessment, having multiple sets of eyes review the results of assessments to ensure that the data collected reflects the score received, and providing the producers we work with numerous opportunities and confidential avenues to provide feedback or concerns related to the execution of the program.

The Impact of Assessments

The need for impartiality is really important because there is a lot on the line when it comes to compliance assessments. Brands use them for internal risk mitigation as well as to make decisions regarding whether to establish a sourcing partnership with a particular producer. Over time, brands will often order fewer goods from producers that demonstrate lower levels of compliance or a lack of improvement in areas deemed uncompliant. To hedge against supply chain disruptions and other risks, brands often source the same (or similar) products from multiple producers. That way, if something disrupts production at one, the brand can quickly increase orders from the other producers to offset any supply shortfalls. If you worked for the brand and one of your producers fell short on compliance standards, would you continue to order from them or—all other factors being equal—opt for one that was performing better?

Another reason CAP results are important is because, depending on the standard system, they may lead to certification or a consumer-facing seal. Certifications and consumer seals are a mark of approval, a way of showing to the world that a particular facility or brand performs high in compliance. Facilities can use certifications and seals to gain new brand clients or demonstrate to responsible sourcing teams that the business meets their requirements. But brands can also use them as a marketing asset to engage consumers. Depending on the way a standard system is structured, brands that source products from certified vendors can put a seal on their hangtags or consumer-facing product web pages to signal their values to customers, who may, in turn, reward those values with their dollars. E-commerce has become so refined that, on many websites, consumers can even filter their product searches for specific sustainability credentials. Many of the certifications you're familiar with, such as Fair Trade, are owned by standard creators who have spent extensive amounts of time and resources on consumer-awareness campaigns so that these seals of approval mean something to the general public.

The Educational Benefit of Compliance

Beyond the risk assessment and assurance, and consumer engagement of certification marks, Nest has found that standards and auditing systems also provide important additional impacts, specifically when it comes to capacity building and skills development. For example, one of our brand partners brought Nest in to work with a vendor in India that they had recently put on probation for failing to comply with the brand's standards. The vendor, a large factory, was struggling to oversee and manage a complicated supply chain of cottage industry embroiders, who were being utilized through a network of subcontractors. The production partner was making the same mistake I mentioned earlier: trying to force their factory-level compliance program into a system where that simply did not make sense. Through partnership with Nest, the factory was able to redirect their efforts toward educating the subcontractors and workers about the importance of compliance and what it means and leverage the Nest program to build the foundational systems of record keeping and worker education that would be needed. The factory explained to the subcontractors and producers that the new compliance processes were not just designed to help the brand but also to create better working conditions for themselves and their fellow producers by ensuring everyone followed the same guidelines and giving them the ability to speak out if those standards were not being met. Once they understood the purpose of the standard and the various guidelines for complying with it, these workers and sub-contractors felt like they had a voice. Fast-forward six months, and the factory was back in good standing with its brand partner, had a clear understanding of its embroidery supply chain (namely, who exactly was actually doing the work and what they were getting paid), and had established whole new avenues of dialogue with those in their supply chain. In addition, everyone understood their rights and responsibilities when it came to making this system work. The embroiderers even began providing suggestions to improve production. For example, they pointed out that, by changing when they received raw materials, they could increase their production efficiency. The focus on education resulted in a win-win-win: the brand felt confident that they were sourcing responsibly, the vendor formed a stronger relationship with both the brand and its produc-ers, and the workers gained a sense of agency as well as the assur-ance that someone (in this case Nest) was watching over them to make sure they were treated fairly.

Ongoing Challenges and Evolution

For all the benefits high-quality standards bring, challenges remain. While the standards systems are critical to increase transparency and corporate responsibility in the supply chain, those involved in supporting them—from the standard-setting organizations to the auditors to the brands to the producers—are still *businesses*. Standard-setting organizations get paid to accredit auditors and receive licensing fees from brands who want to use their consumer-facing labels. Auditing firms get paid to perform audits and report out the findings. Compliant and certified producers get paid by brands who prefer to work with businesses that meet their stand-ards. All of this leads to high levels of competition, which can increase conflicts of interest and move the central mission from worker well-being to firm survival and growth.

Additionally, while this book has described industry standards and best practices, not all standards are designed in this way. There are companies that choose to rely on self-reported data with little or no validation to help decrease the costs of responsible sourcing. In these cases, a production facility has discretion on presenting whether it is operating ethically or sustainably with no third party verifying the accuracy of the statements.

Finally, with a noisy marketing landscape, it is difficult for consumers to know the value of a special seal or certification displayed on a brand's hangtag, website, or packaging, making the investment necessary for true compliance more challenging for retailers to absorb.

Thankfully, as we will explore in a future chapter, advances in technology are making it easier for consumers to retrieve information about the more robust standards, and many companies are becoming increasingly savvy at sharing this information. Soon, you may be able to scan a QR code that takes you directly to the website of a standard-setting organization replete with stories and impact case studies. In some cases, you may even be able to find out exactly *who* produced the item, what they were paid, and when they made it. These are amazing developments that will soon weed out the weaker systems or force them to reevaluate their approaches—allowing consumers to reward additional transparency with additional purchases.

Beyond such efforts to reduce consumer confusion, there are other areas where standards systems continue to improve and refine. It used to be common practice that brands would take a "three strikes and you're out" mentality when it came to the compliance of their production partners. This meant that the producer would have three chances to hit a perfect score on their audit, and if they failed to do so, the brand would drop them (either temporarily or permanently) as a supplier. Think for a moment about the unintended consequences of this type of requirement. It incentivizes producers to sweep any potential issues under the rug, hiding them from their brand partners instead of openly discussing the challenges they face in staying compliant. The producer, when feeling the pressure of lost business, may also engage in unethical behavior—like bribing an auditor to ignore any issues they find. All of this creates a culture that rewards passing the audit instead of addressing systemic challenges. It also gives brands virtually all the power while factories face all the responsibility for ethical sourcing, creating a dynamic that is ultimately unsustainable.

Thankfully, this dynamic is starting to change. Many brands are revising their strategies and systems to ensure relationship building and shared responsibility are at the heart of their systems. As a result, most corporations have now pivoted their responsible sourcing models to focus on continuous improvement over time. Think of the preceding example, where a brand chose to work with Nest and its production partners to improve compliance rather than dropping the partner completely, leading to an understanding of the root causes of noncompliance and a collaborative solution to the challenges and thus a trust-based production relationship. Within this type of approach, producers are encouraged to be vocal about challenges they are facing, working together with both the brand and often the standard-setting organization to address them. Standard-setting organizations have focused more energy and attention on solving problems, and brands have supported these efforts by sharing in the cost or partnering with additional NGOs to help address systemic issues, such as financial literacy or unsafe conditions.

A third issue that used to be pervasive within the auditing sector was the fact that different brands required different standards. If you ever talk to anyone in the responsible sourcing, standards, or auditing sectors, they will all be familiar with the fable of the three fire extinguishers. This is the type of story that gets told at every conference pertaining to compliance to the point that it has become cliché. As the story goes, one day a brand representative was visiting a factory when they noticed three fire extinguishers placed at different heights on the same column. Wondering why a single factory would need access to three extinguishers in the exact same place, the representative asked the owner about it. "Well," the owner said, "your company requires the extinguisher to be set at one height, but another brand we work with requires a different height. A third brand requires another height. For my facility to maintain a perfect compliance score, it is easier for me to just place three extinguishers on the same column than have to move them around every time there is an audit."

This story highlights two issues that many production partners face. On the one hand, there can be confusion surrounding different standards for different partners. On the other, it illustrates how often factories experience audit fatigue: if each brand they work with requires a different standard and they are being audited almost all the time, then they need to hire teams of people to merely keep up with the demands of constant audits. Within the apparel sector, the Sustainable Apparel Coalition (SAC),[2] an industry effort consisting of over 100 brands, realized that many brands were sourcing from the same businesses but demanding different compliance requirements, leading to issues like the one highlighted above. As a result, the SAC launched two efforts, the HIGG Index (whose name was inspired by the Higgs boson search) and the Social Labor Convergence Project (SLCP). In both of these initiatives, the goal is to create one single comprehensive audit for environmental (HIGG) concerns and social/labor (SCLP) concerns. The current iteration of these tools is an audit document containing thousands of questions, as each brand contributed their own data needs into the greater whole.

As I write this in 2022, the HIGG Index is experiencing some controversy as critics (including both nations such as Norway and participating brands such as H&M)[3] have pointed out various shortcomings. For instance, critics point out that the methodology favors the use of synthetic materials (e.g. recycled polyester), which has been proven to have negative consequences for the environment. Secondly, the SAC has not shared with outside groups how the HIGG is scored.[4] Finally, the methodology lacks a full life-cycle analysis,[5] which means that brands get rewarded for utilizing recycled materials, but no one asks what happens to those garments after the consumer is done with them. Does the brand simply delay the garment material's journey to the landfill, or does it create more of a cradle-to-cradle (vs. cradle-to-grave) solution? As a result of this controversy, the SAC has paused the use of the HIGG while it conducts an independent analysis of the index. Still, I believe this current crisis will only serve to strengthen the index and have faith that, over time, the SAC will develop something more viable, enabling producers to spend three or four days per year dealing with one audit instead of hundreds of days dealing with a countless number coming from each individual brand. It is an example of the industry coming together to work on a system challenge; of course there will be some stumbles along the way.

Finally, there are continuing issues with the practice of auditing. As audit firms grow larger and have a more significant global reach, it becomes increasingly difficult to monitor the activities of everyone on the global auditing team. Each firm is only as good as their worst auditor. Turnover, improper training, and lack of cultural competency can drastically impact the success of an audit. To address this risk, the auditing community has embraced both technology and industry collaboration. Firstly, technology has advanced, allowing firms to have geo-location tags on their auditors, thus confirming an auditor's exact location when they are performing their work. Are you in the field, observing independent farmers, or are you at the local cantina? In addition, the auditing community has come together forming organizations that provide oversight over the auditors themselves, ensuring the validity of their findings but also reinforcing their methodology through training and accreditation.

Shifting to Root Causes and Shared Ownership

By now you should have a better sense of the mechanics behind supply chain transparency and the tools utilized by the responsible sourcing team, alongside some of the positive impacts (and pressures) that result from auditing and standards. There is certainly still work to do in order to strengthen the system, and as the next chapter will show, the wheels still do fall off the cart in ways that can lead to tragic impacts. However, it is encouraging to know that the industry as a whole is increasingly focused on root causes and shared ownership.

5

Wake-Up Calls: The Dual Disasters of Rana Plaza and COVID-19

"There is a saying in Tibetan, 'Tragedy should be utilized as a source of strength.'
No matter what sort of difficulties, how painful experience is, if we lose our hope, that's our real disaster."

—Dalai Lama XIV

THANKS TO AN increased interest in and awareness of responsible sourcing over the past 30 years, the global production community has come a long way since the Nike soccer ball scandal of the 1990s. However, simply because systems for increased transparency and accountability have been created and are now utilized, supply chains remain complex, and the models do not always operate the way we would hope. Over the last several years, our world has shifted in ways that have brought new global challenges but also new technologies and opportunities. These shifts can result from economic crises, natural disasters, political unrest, consumer demand, and the myriad other events that can impact a globalized supply chain. Meanwhile, the industry has also continued to learn from existing solutions. These changes and learnings require brands to continually reevaluate and improve their approach to sourcing and supply chains, as well as the tools they use to ensure that they and their sourcing partners are operating responsibly.

In this chapter we will look at two disruptive events that highlighted weaknesses within the responsible-sourcing sector. Both events have led to a concerted effort to address industry-wide, systemic shortcomings that affect how goods continue to be produced and sourced. Specifically, we will look at the Rana Plaza factory collapse of 2013, as well as the more recent (and, as I write this, ongoing) COVID-19 pandemic. In both cases, we will explore not only the weaknesses these tragedies exposed but, more importantly, *why* they disrupted global sourcing strategy and *how* the brands and producers affected have responded in ways that ultimately will improve our supply chains.

The Tragedy at Rana Plaza

On the morning of April 24, 2013, the busy streets of Dhaka, Bangladesh, were shaken by the sound of mass destruction. The Rana Plaza Factory, an eight-story building in the Savar Upazila district, collapsed. This was not the result of an explosion, a terrorist attack, or an earthquake; the building had succumbed to structural failure. By the time the search for survivors was called off on May 13, 1,134 of the 3,122 garment workers who had been in the building had lost their lives, and an additional 2,500 were injured (including several bystanders who were on the street outside at the time of the collapse). It was the deadliest garment-industry accident in recorded history.[1] To make matters even more devastating, this was a preventable tragedy, the result of multiple points of failure and a stark example of the negative consequences of unfettered globalization combined with a lack of regulatory oversight and enforcement.

The day before the collapse, cracks in the walls and columns of the building began to appear and, out of fear, many workers fled the building. The management team called in an engineer, who informed them that the cracks indicated the building was dangerously unstable. However, the next morning, the factory owner and management told workers that they had met with government officials and determined the building was not an imminent risk. They promised that a more thorough structural assessment would be performed at a later date. Workers at a bank located on the ground floor of the building heeded the first warning and closed shop until repairs were made. However, the factory owner sent a clear message to all his workers on the remaining floors: if they did not show up to work, they would lose their jobs.[2] In a country of steep unemployment and brutal poverty, what choice did these workers have?

As rescue workers sifted through the rubble and global news networks covered the events, it was not just images of the dead and injured that came into focus. Among the destruction, cameras captured glimpses of garments and labels of well-known brands. Responding to the devastation, as well as questions about the role they played in the tragedy, many of these brands claimed they didn't know their clothing was being manufactured at this factory.[3] How could this be? Evidently, this was not only a humanitarian crisis, but a wake-up call over the lack of transparency and accountability within the international garment industry.

Over the next years of investigations that followed the disaster, a few key issues became clear. First, Bangladesh lacked adequate building and fire standards, with almost no regulatory oversight from the government. This particular factory was originally built as a four-story building, but four illegally constructed floors were added later, and a fifth was under construction at the time of collapse. The foundation of the structure was literally built on sand, as the area was a former lakebed. And, to make matters worse, the support columns utilized inferior materials and did not account for the extreme weight of heavy machinery that was being utilized on the higher floors.[4] From the start, this was a recipe for disaster, but it was also not uncommon; the same shoddy construction could be found in countless buildings and factories across the city as well. The government was turning a blind eye, afraid to disrupt an industry that provided a significant amount of GDP for the country as well as millions of stable, albeit low-paying, jobs to a largely unemployed country struggling under the weight of poverty.

Second, while the lack of government regulation was distressing, brands and retailers were relying on these systems rather than building and enforcing their own. This was confounded by issues discussed in the last chapter regarding compliance systems. Brands claimed to not know their products were being produced at this facility due to subcontracting practices that allowed regulated factories to outsource portions of their production to other, unregulated facilities. This left brands without transparency or oversight into their full supply chain.

Let's look more closely at what happened and why.

Why Bangladesh?

For many reasons, the fact that this tragedy occurred in Bangladesh was less a surprise and more of a testament to unchecked globalization and the imbalance of power between brands and production partners. Just as Mexico's economy had benefited from NAFTA, Bangladesh had become an unexpected superpower within garment production as a result of another US government trade agreement: the 1974 Multi-Fiber Arrangement. This legislation established quotas on the textiles that could be exported from emerging economies to first-world countries. This heavily impacted the large textile and garment manufacturing industries in China, Hong Kong, Korea, and India, but Bangladesh was not included in the agreement. As a result, importer countries placed no tariffs or quotas on the garment exports coming from that country. This competitive advantage led to explosive growth within Bangladesh's existing garment industry. Between 1978 and 2012, almost unbelievably, Bangladesh went from $43,608/year (adjusted for inflation) to $21 billion/year in garment exports![5] By 2010 the garment industry accounted for 12% of the country's GDP, and by 2013 textiles made up 80% of all exports from the country.[6] Not only did it become a key driver of the economy, but it also became a source of higher-quality jobs as well. Even though from a global perspective the wages earned in Bangladesh were far below the averages in other countries (the 2012 average for a garment worker in Bangladesh was $61 per month, compared with China where it was $389 per month), the garment industry still provided a better-paying job than most in the country (the 2012 minimum wage was only $42 per month). Twelve percent of all women between the ages of 15 and 30 were employed by the sector,[7] and that number was continuing to rise.

But the explosive growth came at a cost, and the government and industry struggled as a result. The construction industry could not build new manufacturing facilities quickly enough to fulfill demand. To keep up, construction companies employed substandard building practices and materials, which went unchecked by building-safety regulations and oversight. Although the government had the authority and responsibility to intervene, it could not keep pace and, perhaps, was inclined to ignore possible issues in order to keep the economy humming. The Bangladesh Garment Manufacturers for Export Association (BGMEA), which owned the factories, was also responsible for auditing the safety of those factories.[8] Pondering this fact, I can't help but think of the famous quote from the Roman poet Juvenal, *Quis custodiet ipsos custodes?* "Who watches the watchers?" In addition, Bangladeshi factories catered to high-volume, low-margin business partners and thus faced pressure to boost production while lowering costs year over year. Even if they wanted to improve conditions, operating under such low margin they often did not have the capital to make the improvements. The government itself, where corruption was rampant, was also not incentivized to strengthen these systems, as it did not want to disrupt the major growth industry for the country or the businesses that were lining its pockets. In many cases, it actively sought to undermine efforts of unionization, and while it supported NGO projects around financial literacy and women's empowerment, it did not allow nonprofit or third-party auditors coming in to snoop around the factories, leaving many issues undiagnosed and invisible.

Illegal Subcontracting

The lack of governmental oversight was compounded by another issue: that of illegal subcontracting. It is important to note that even if brands had been successful in engaging independent audits, they still would not have exposed the issues of Rana Plaza. The fact is that, until their labels were found in the rubble of the factory, most brands had no idea their products were being made there. Most corporate social responsibility programs of the time focused solely on "Tier One" factories, the first and primary point of production for a brand's items. When factories exceed capacity, it's common practice for them to partner with a second nearby facility to share production. This can be done with the brand's consent and participation, but since that consent requires the secondary facility to undergo the same, often rigorous and expensive, oversight, many factories had begun doing this without the brands consent or knowledge. Rana Plaza was one of these invisible subcontractors in their supply chains. This is a complex issue. While the fault should certainly lie squarely with the company engaged by the brand to produce its items, this subcontracting often happens due to the unrealistic demands of the brand to speed up production while lowering cost.

Weaknesses Exposed, and What to Do About Them

As you can see, while this governmental ecosystem within Bangladesh was certainly conducive to a disaster like that of Rana Plaza, the tragedy also made many in the industry realize that brands needed to acknowledge their role in the issue. It is important to remember that at the time of Rana Plaza, there were already strong compliance standards systems in use around the world. The Fair Labor Association had already been in existence since 1999, and Social Accountability International since 1997—these are just two examples. However, *how* the standards were being used and assessed, and the nature of the relationship between brands and suppliers, also helped lay the groundwork for the disaster. The often-combative business relationships did not incentivize dialogue or disclosure from their vendor partners, instead having them ignore or hide problems in order to focus on delivering orders and competing with other vendors on price. The brands' emphasis on cost above all else led to corners being cut in building and fire safety, not to mention workers' wages and their overall well-being. The brands also did not engage nearly enough at the worker level, and combined with the difficulty in unionization, brands did not provide any avenues for workers to express their concerns or complaints. Remember, the workers at Rana Plaza saw the cracks and knew something was wrong; they just did not have any power to do anything about it. All these problems compounded because brands did not work together to address these issues; everyone was working in isolation instead of raising awareness of systemic issues and tackling them collaboratively. The traditional practice of just checking boxes for compliance, without real partnership with vendors to address root causes for problems found (that "three strikes and you are out" mentality mentioned in Chapter 4), meant that things were bound to get worse, not better. The industry was complicit in perpetuating the problem, and if nothing was done, there was going to be another Rana Plaza. And while Bangladesh was a likely place for this tragedy to be repeated due to the weak government regulations, lack of oversight, and complete reliance on low-margin production, there are many other countries where dangers were going equally as unchecked.

The international outrage in response to the Rana Plaza tragedy meant that any brands who sourced products from Bangladesh needed to respond. They had a few options to consider. Firstly, as cynical as it sounds, they could choose to do nothing and wait out the bad press with the hope that their customers would stay loyal after the firestorm passed. There was some logic here, as consumer surveys indicated that not many people were planning on changing their shopping behavior based on how brands addressed the issue of Rana Plaza. In fact, in a May 2013 consumer survey from Retail Week, 44% of those surveyed said that the factory collapse had made no difference in whether consumers would ask retailers about where the clothes they bought were produced (7% indicated they had not heard about the collapse, and another 14% said they were not sure).[9] Secondly, they could opt to stop sourcing from Bangladesh altogether. The downside to that approach would be that the same brands who had helped create the conditions under which the Rana Plaza tragedy took place would then do nothing to help address these root causes, and the removal of business from the country would further weaken the national economy. It would also require corporations to rebuild supply chains from the ground up, causing production delays and other organizational challenges. And finally, brands could consider working together alongside the factories and government to address the challenges. Understandably, this thought led to some trepidation given the monumental task required. Early estimates from the Worker Rights Consortium, an independent labor rights organization, predicted that the cost to improve conditions in the 5,000 garment factories would average $600,000 per factory, or approximately $3 billion overall.[10] And a stronger system of auditing, accountability, and oversight would certainly need to be established, which would take years and significant effort and collaboration from a multitude of partners. Even with the potential price tag and heavy lift required, for most brands it was this last option that they embarked upon. Just as Nike made the decision to acknowledge its responsibility in the conditions under which its products were made, corporations began to acknowledge their role in creating a system that enabled Rana Plaza to happen, and many made commitments to work together in order to do better. I firmly believe that the lasting impacts of this important choice laid the groundwork for continued innovations in responsible sourcing still being felt today, including Nest's ability to establish a Steering Committee to address supply chain transparency for homeworkers and small workshops.

Collaboration as a Force for Good

This tragedy spurred a dramatic shift within the retail industry toward collaboration with a common purpose. As a result, two different large-scale, multi-stakeholder efforts quickly emerged: The Bangladesh Fire and Safety Accord[11] and The Alliance for Bangladesh Worker Safety.[12] Between the two, more than 100 brands participated. The Accord was composed primarily of European brands, alongside two Bangladeshi unions, and set forth a five-year plan to improve fire and safety conditions in the factories of Bangladesh. The retail members of the Accord absorbed partial financial responsibility of the needed repairs, agreeing to a maximum of $2.5 million per brand over the course of those five years. In addition, to address the issue of a lack of oversight, independent inspection organizations audited factories, and the Accord published findings of any safety issues for all to see. By 2014, the Accord had found 80,000 safety hazards across the 1,100 factories covered in the agreement.[13] The trade unions, who historically had been repressed by the Bangladeshi government, were granted a seat on the board of the Accord to help steer its leadership and direction. Finally, the Accord required that all parties agreed to enter into a legally binding agreement with the trade unions that allowed the unions to make claims against any brands that failed to meet their obligations within the Accord. This final requirement, while important, resulted in very few US-based firms joining that effort. These firms then created the Alliance as an alternative. Unlike in Europe, the United States does not cap the amount of financial damages that parties can pursue through class-action lawsuits, and many of the US brands felt that opening themselves up to lawsuits presented too high a risk. Under the Alliance, all responsibility to comply with safety standards falls to the factory owners. In addition, the funding required by each brand member was smaller: $1 million instead of the $2.5 million, augmented by the availability of $100 million in loans through agencies such as the International Finance Corporation for factories to fund any needed repairs.

While slightly different in their approaches, both the Accord and the Alliance significantly increased industry collaboration, creating new models for greater accountability within the auditing process, sharing valuable information related to risk, and taking ownership to help address root causes. More recent establishments of collaborative efforts, such as the Sustainable Apparel Coalition or the Zero Waste Pledge, can trace their origins back to this pivotal moment in 2013. After the five years of the stated agreement, the work of the Alliance ended. However, the work of the Accord has continued to expand. In August 2021, it officially became a global effort, changing its name to The International Accord for Health and Safety in the Textile and Garment Industry, with a membership of more than 175 brands. The Accord has been largely considered a success: thousands of factories have installed better safety mechanisms, wages and labor conditions have started to improve, and over 300 factories that did not demonstrate a willingness to improve have been blacklisted. Is there still room to improve? Absolutely. But what these collaborative efforts have accomplished has certainly altered the course of doing business.

Wake-Up Call #2: COVID-19

The COVID-19 pandemic has impacted every corner of the globe, resulting in the deaths of millions and changing life as we know it.

As I write this, we continue to learn about new strains of the virus and expect that this illness will be with us for the foreseeable future. While the impacts of COVID-19 are vast, it has highlighted both continued inequity within supply chains and an increased realization that the complexity of our production models poses significant risk. The Rana Plaza disaster had more easily identified root causes and felt geographically finite. The COVID-19 pandemic not only shattered the belief that we could anticipate all risk, but it also highlighted the global instability we will face from future crises, whether it's climate change, future pandemics, or something else we can't foresee. As a result, COVID-19 has forced us to reevaluate the standard business and operating model for brands sourcing products from around the world.

COVID-19 in Supply Chains

As an organization, Nest was moments away from inking a 10-year lease agreement on a new office location in Manhattan in early March 2020. Like many, as the news reports confirmed the first case of COVID-19 in New York City, where we're headquartered, we began discussing the likelihood of a citywide shutdown. Shortly after the city closed public schools the third week into the month, we decided to not only hold off on signing a new lease but to close our Bryant Park offices as well. "It's temporary" we all thought, as the Nest team took some personal items and paperwork home, expecting to be back in the office in a few weeks. As weeks turned to months, we—along with the rest of the world—realized this strange illness was going to be more disruptive than anyone thought.

If this uncertainty was taking place in New York, in a country with strong infrastructure and support networks, what was happening to the homeworkers and artisans whom we served as an organization? What were the downstream impacts from the massive closure of nonessential retail? Every call and town hall meeting with Nest's stakeholders told us the same story: brands were abruptly cancelling orders, most of which were already in production if not fully completed. Payment to the production partners virtually stopped. Brands were going on furlough, shuttering their businesses for the foreseeable future, leaving downstream production partners wondering how they would survive. In our case, most of these handcraft businesses offered the only source of income for the women and men engaged in producing the goods, providing extremely valuable income for the families and communities with which the businesses worked. Think again about Laurie in the Philippines. Her income fed her children, purchased their school clothes, and helped Laurie and her family absorb economic shocks such as unexpected illnesses or poor crop production without long-term negative consequences. This was not an artisan problem: this was happening to factories and production centers around the world. Estimates from the #PayUp campaign, which urged brands to pay their contractors in the early days of the pandemic, indicated that upwards of $40 billion worth of orders were canceled around the world in 2020.[14]

In addition to the negative impact the pandemic had on workers and their family finances, remember that most production happens in emerging economies, where access to adequate health and social services is difficult, if not impossible, for the vulnerable or poor. These countries were the least equipped to weather a global pandemic. They lacked enough hospital beds, respirators, PPE, or frankly any sort of social security, worker's compensation, or insurance. Seeing the stark contrast between how relatively privileged people and those from more disadvantaged backgrounds experienced the pandemic, perhaps it was only natural that consumers, NGOs, and businesses themselves started asking a critical question:

what responsibility did a brand have to those workers on the other side of the world?

Opportunity out of Crisis

Unsurprisingly, many of the brands that accepted more responsibility for their supply chains after events like the Nike scandal and Rana Plaza disaster were the same ones that chose *not* to cancel orders despite COVID-19's impact on their business. Instead, they held up their end of their agreements and paid the businesses they worked with for the orders. For brands without more self-driven accountability, consumer activism kicked in: campaigns such as the aforementioned #PayUp social media campaign publicly shamed brands for their lack of responsibility, demonstrating the impact of their order cancelations and pressuring them to fulfill their financial obligations. Within the first two years of its existence, the #PayUp campaign was responsible for getting 25 major global clothing brands to repay $22 billion worth of orders they had canceled at the start of the pandemic.[15]

Responsible brands also knew that, with such uncertainty in the market, it was going to be extremely difficult to predict future order volumes. As such, they would not be able keep their production partners afloat through purchasing alone. Instead, they began to leverage corporate philanthropy to support businesses in other ways. For example, at Nest many of our handcraft partners had started sewing masks for their communities once orders for traditional products stopped coming. They were not getting paid for these; they were making them and donating them because they knew their communities needed them. In a matter of weeks, Nest was able to raise over $1 million in corporate philanthropy to provide grants to these businesses to keep doing what they were doing.

This enabled them to pay their craft workers proper wages all while creating and donating thousands of units of PPE to both global communities and to the United States Postal Service, the residents of New York City Public Housing, and for essential workers in 18 countries. This utilization of philanthropy was a lifeline both for the producer businesses and their workers but also the community at large. It also illustrated a major positive shift in how brands approach their relationship to their production partners.

Brands also used philanthropy to support global efforts to deliver vaccines, health care, and other emergency services to communities in need. Many larger corporations made significant commitments to combatting the pandemic. Microsoft donated $55 million to help nonprofits provide medical relief and disseminate accurate information.[16] Target donated $1 million to support the purchase of medical equipment and supplies around the world through partnerships with organizations such as UNICEF, Project ECHO, and the World Health Organization Solidarity Response Fund.[17] In many ways, this brand behavior was reflective of the declaration made by Larry Fink from Blackrock: brands and corporations have an increased responsibility to people and planet, as governments have shown that they are unable to single-handedly manage social and environmental crises. Brands should be leading the way in their behavior and supporting the efforts (via nonprofits and international agencies) to combat the negative impacts of issues such as COVID-19.

Supply Chain Resiliency and Diversity

COVID-19 has accelerated thinking and action in a few other key categories. Firstly, every brand—no matter how large or small—is now keenly focused on supply chain resiliency and how sourcing partners, and brands themselves, prepare for unexpected shocks.

With climate change impacts steadily increasing worldwide, this work was already under way. But while climate change concerns had inspired the initial conversations and planning around resiliency, COVID-19 rapidly accelerated the discussion while also introducing new variables. This was primarily because the pandemic shut down so many different aspects of the supply chain, whereas most climate change planning anticipated regionally isolated disruptions caused by major disasters in specific geographic areas. But because COVID-19 affected the whole world, it touched all corners of the supply chain. Raw materials were no longer accessible. Factories were no longer in operation due to government shutdowns (first in China and then globally). Shipping ground to a halt when ports were closed. One study by Resilinc indicated that many months after the first COVID-19 cases were reported, more than 70% of brands were still trying to map their China-based supply chains.[18] The reality is that with so many different actors, getting the actual supply chain information is really difficult and often relies more on anecdotal evidence than true boots on the ground.

COVID-19 also shifted the way brands thought about sourcing and further reinforced the idea that brands must focus on factors other than simply getting products to the shelf as quickly and as cheaply as possible. The major global disruptions further indicated that retailers must also consider all aspects of sustainability, including precisely where production is happening (even when it is outside of a factory) and how to ensure all key production partners are prepared for disasters. The pandemic encouraged brands to proactively work with their producers as true partners, helping them figure out how to counter-source raw materials or plan for other unexpected disruptions in the future. Some brands donated brain power (in the form of internal brand teams) to work with their vendors to create resiliency strategies and counter-sourcing opportunities. Others provided capital to outfit factories with newer production systems that were less reliant on outdated methods or technologies, which could be converted into new lines of production should raw materials need to change or products to shift quickly to meet an immediate societal need.

COVID-19 has also impacted brand thinking around the concept of homeworkers. Due to the complications and fear of subcontracting discussed earlier in this chapter, many brands have strict policies in this regard. This fear is often compounded when the subcontracting includes home-based workers given the further difficulty in bringing transparency to a dispersed and cottage industry workforce. This was the origin and need for the development of the Nest Standard for Homes and Small Workshops. Despite the growth of Nest's program, there are still many brands that have maintained antiquated no-homeworker policies within their codes of conduct out of residual fear. Such policies prohibit vendors from using workers outside of the formal factory system. However, COVID-19 required all of us—from production partners to corporate headquarters—to work from home. For many companies who had not yet considered the Nest program, this required them to reconsider the strict pre-pandemic policies. Our work helping retailers update their internal policies and communicate to their vendors that it was now permissible to consider home-based labor production rapidly expanded. Not only did this allow the factory workers who had been sent home to continue working, it also gave factory owners the ability to subcontract to home-based workers who had previously been forbidden from participation.

There was another root cause for this change in attitude toward homeworkers and more artisanal production: the shift in consumer interest and behavior. As everyone remained home-bound, hearing stories of the bravery of frontline workers alongside the brand-shaming of the #PayUp campaign, consumers had greater time to learn and engage online. This led to an increase in consumer engagement around the impact of their purchasing decisions. Among those surveyed, 69% of Gen Zs said they would pay more for a product if the employees and suppliers who helped produce that product are treated fairly.[19] While there is certainly social desirability bias in those surveys, the trend is also clear. This also dovetailed with the rise of consumer, worker, and social-justice activism in the wake of the murders of Breonna Taylor and George Floyd and other Black men and women in the Spring of 2020 launching the national, and ultimately international, Black Lives Matter Movement. The increased awareness surrounding the plight of communities of color in the United States and other majority-white nations gave rise to increased calls for corporate accountability and financial support of businesses run by Black, Indigenous, and People of Color (BIPOC). From a brand perspective this awareness gave rise to various diversity and equity commitments, including the launch of a collaborative 15% Pledge (a commitment to stock 15% of their shelf space from BIPOC-owned businesses) and an effort to diversify their boards, leadership teams, and workforces.

Given the uncertainty in the world, overconsumption started to lose some of its appeal. Perhaps the first to feel this shift was the luxury fashion space, where there was a 40% decrease in value of luxury brands in the span of just three months in 2020.[20] In a sector that relied on constant "newness" with multiple seasonal collections each year, brands such as Gucci decided to start focusing more on longer-term, seasonless collections for their customers (something sustainability advocates have been pushing for decades!). If this trend holds, there could be potential ripple-effect impacts into the world of fast fashion as well, since such a large part of that business model involves replicating runway looks from high-fashion brands. These seasonless collections, combined with the rise of fashion rental platforms such as Rent the Runway, speak to the growing consumer interest in reducing overall consumption and slowing down the speed to which retail had kept pace. And with this slow down, artisanship and craft—which by definition takes longer and more care to produce—are finding a whole new audience. Handcraft is starting to reclaim market share it had been steadily losing since the advent of mass manufacturing and industrialization. Research & Markets indicates that the global handcraft sector is now expected to reach $984.8 billion by the end of 2023, expanding at a compound annual growth rate (CAGR) of more than 11% during 2018–2023.[21]

What's Next

The wake-up calls spurred by events such as Rana Plaza and COVID-19 highlight how attitudes and behaviors toward responsible sourcing continue to improve over time. Social issues, economic crises, disasters, consumer awareness, consumption habits—all of these things affect brand behavior. And as shifts occur and we look for ways to insulate against risks both predictable and not, brands will continue to evolve. Just as in natural evolutionary processes, the brands will need to continue to change by becoming more collaborative, sustainable, and resilient because if they do not, they will eventually become irrelevant and have no way to survive. These are, ultimately, businesses that need to remain profitable in order to exist, but as Larry Fink said, businesses have to consider the impact of their choices or face extinction.

6

Walking Further Together: Partnership and Innovation

"If you want to go fast, go alone. If you want to go far, go together."
—African Proverb

By now, you might be throwing your hands up in the air and thinking that responsible sourcing seems all too complicated. With so many risks lurking behind every decision, how can anyone figure out the best way to operate? If the whole exercise feels a little hopeless, don't fret! To be successful in responsible sourcing and corporate social responsibility, you are going to need some help, and thankfully, increasingly, that help is available. This is where partnerships, collaboration, and innovation come in.

While we talked in previous chapters about the emergence of industry coalitions (such as the efforts that resulted from the Rana Plaza tragedy), in this chapter we will look at how brands form successful partnerships with other companies (sometimes competitors), as well as nonprofits and NGOs, to create a win-win-win situation: a symbiotic relationship that benefits *both* partners and—and this is key—the supply chains within which the brands work. These types of partnerships have proven successful in improving sustainable sourcing and increasing positive societal impacts while simultaneously generating investor and consumer interest through the free publicity gained by media reporting. For example, the Adidas and Allbirds collaboration, which we will explore later in this chapter, has received coverage from CNN, Vogue Business, Newsweek, The Daily Beast, and many other outlets, thus driving massive consumer interest in a partnership formed with sustainability at its heart. As a result of all the upside potential, there is an astounding amount of innovation and bold investments being made in this sector, much of which is rooted in partnership models. This energy is forming a virtuous circle: the rise in attention is spurring new business approaches and technologies that are then translating into new opportunities for responsible sourcing and supply chain impacts.

What Forms a Strong Partnership

Before diving into some examples of powerful partnerships, it is important to think about what ingredients are necessary to encourage successful collaborative action. In 2014, the *Harvard Business Review* published an article, which remains extremely influential today, entitled "The Collaboration Imperative,"[1] which outlines exactly that. In our own experience at Nest, collaborating with brands and production partners, we have found the article's findings to be extremely insightful.

- **Start small but committed.** Find a few key partners that are "all in" on working together to find a solution for the challenge at hand. For Nest, this took the form of our partnerships with West Elm, Patagonia, and Target during the earliest days of our effort to develop a compliance program. Keeping the collaboration small at the start allowed us to create a pathway forward with a smaller number of voices and needs at the table. For us this meant ensuring we were all aligned about the problem we were looking to solve, confirming there was a true need from the market, and forming a strategy to attack the issue. If you start with too many voices or stakeholders, it is more difficult to build consensus and stay focused. Another thing we agreed on was the commitment to bring others on board once we articulated and aligned on a clear goal. Because our brand partners all had very strong industry track records of investment in solutions, this was relatively easy. With their help, Eileen Fisher, PVH (the fashion corporation that owns Phillips-Van Heusen, Tommy Hilfiger, Calvin Klein, and many others), and The

Children's Place quickly joined the effort, along with countless advisors and a number of handcraft-business leaders.

- **Think through additional stakeholder inclusion.** Once your
  small but mighty group is ready to get started, engage multiple
  points of view in order to create the most comprehensive
  solution, as well as laying the groundwork for widespread
  adoption. Are there critical strategic partnerships required to
  implement the solution? Invite those parties to the table.
  What about potential roadblocks? You need to tread carefully,
  but including some potential challengers to your process early
  on may help address their concerns and result in a stronger
  initiative. This also provides an opportunity to form unlikely
  alliances and potentially convert people to your cause. In the
  case of Nest, we knew we needed to include retailers but also
  the handcraft producer businesses themselves, since they
  would bring a very different point of view. In addition, since
  Nest was not founded as a compliance organization, we
  needed auditing and standard-setting expertise within our
  effort. Did everyone we ask join the initiative? Of course not.
  But we were lucky enough to gather a group of equally
  weighted, diverse voices and areas of expertise to create a program and solution that met the needs of all. In addition to
  brands and production partners, we consulted with the auditing firm Bureau Veritas, the standard-setting organization
  Social Accountability International, and the Center for Sustainable Business at the NYU Stern School of Business, to
  name just a few.
- **Link self-interest with shared interest.** All right, so you
  have the members in place and are actively working toward a
  solution. How can you ensure that you do not lose momentum and your initiative continues to make progress? It is
  important to establish a safe space for brands and other

stakeholders to engage without worrying that other members will steal ideas or opportunities. (The parties are often competitors after all.) All parties must understand that a successful initiative means everyone benefits. Steer clear of specific business or market strategies and focus more on solutions that would help everyone: cutting costs, reducing risks, or even increasing margin. By utilizing the "rising tide lifts all boats" mentality, your effort will be more likely to promote dialogue among participants. During our effort at Nest, we employed what is known as *Chatham House Rules* for our Steering Committee meetings, which meant any confidential information shared during the course of our meetings would not leave the room. This enabled brands and producers alike to be more honest about challenges and concerns. Additionally, our members set the tone very early on, with brands that normally competed with one another coming together to tackle a challenge they all shared—monitoring homeworking in their supply chains—so they were goal-oriented and focused. This was not a place for companies to be protective of their intellectual property, and sticking to ground rules helped assure members of this. If there were sensitivities related to specific producers, brand partners were not required to disclose to the entire group the names and locations of their sourcing partners, and by signing robust non-disclosure agreements with everyone, Nest signaled we would also keep any information they were sensitive about confidential unless given permission to do otherwise.

- **Build in healthy competition.** While a safe space is necessary, you can still leverage competition in productive ways. Brands naturally want to stay abreast of what their competitors are doing, and they want to be able to boast about being the best in their sector. A good way to do this without pitting brands against each other is to set benchmarks and measure progress so members know how they are doing compared to the others in tackling the same or similar problems. For example, as the Nest program launched, we reported to the Steering Committee the number of supply chains each member was enrolling into the program, as well as the number of workers who were positively impacted for each member, and we tracked how many production partners for each brand were becoming certified (or deemed high performing). We designed these activities to encourage the companies that were already working hard to stay motivated and to nudge the members that were lagging behind. Early adopters are important as they can encourage wider industry adoption once the effort is officially launched.

Other NGO Partnerships

Nest's work is just one example of how brands can work with nonprofits or NGOs to increase their impact and sustainability. There are several reasons why a brand might choose to partner with an NGO. Firstly, nonprofits are, by definition, mission-driven organizations, established to meet a specific and defined societal need. So, if you are a corporation that is seeking to solve a particular challenge, it is very appealing to partner with a nonprofit that was founded, and has built expertise and experience, to address that very need.

Because nonprofits are mission focused and profits are not shared with investors or shareholders, there is also an assumption that they will offer their services at a better price than a for-profit company. Margin can certainly be baked into their pricing model (and should be from a financial sustainability perspective), but nonprofits are generally more focused on system-wide solutions than they are on solely generating revenue. This is very much the approach we took at Nest when pricing our compliance program. As we were (and still are) the only standards and auditing program for production occurring in homes and small workshops, filling a rather gaping hole in the sector, we could have, in theory, charged significantly more than we do. However, as our goal is to encourage greater market access for artisan and handcraft businesses through the increased supply chain transparency our program promotes, we wanted to be sure the price point was accessible while still covering our costs and overheads. Better to have 50 brands engage with us at a lower price than charge two a much higher fee in exchange for way less impact.

Grant funders typically require nonprofits to provide extensive reporting on how they use their funding and the impact it has had. As such, nonprofits are often experts at creating systems to monitor and collect key performance indicators (KPIs) and other metrics as part of their operations. This is another benefit that brands receive from nonprofit partnership: the organization collects and provides both metrics and rich qualitative storytelling elements so that the employees who manage the relationship can be armed with outcomes and impact stories to share with their bosses and investors. At Nest, we often talk to our brand partners before starting a scope of work in order to understand what the corporation might be interested in leveraging: for example, how could the data plug into internal tracking toward corporate sustainability goals? Or toward the United Nations Sustainable Development Goals (UNSDGs)? Are they keenly focused on gender dynamics and as such would want us to independently track the performance of female stakeholders versus male stakeholders? Or in the case of Nest's compliance work, and likely many other similar initiatives, industry benchmarking can also be provided so that the brand can understand how its supply chain is performing compared to the rest of the industry and the level of impact that brand is having versus industry averages. This is all work that the nonprofit is willing and able to do for its brand partner.

A final benefit to partnering with a nonprofit has to do with external signaling. By partnering and publicizing the work externally, a brand can leverage the reputation of that nonprofit to help boost its own reputation in the market. We will talk about greenwashing in a future chapter, but in this case, I am referring to authentic partnerships working to address a real need and creating solutions that will eventually be shared throughout the industry. Through its strategic partnership, the brand is demonstrating its commitment in solving these challenges and is thus able to benefit from that reputation.[2]

Risks to Consider in Nonprofit Partnerships

Although there are obvious benefits to working with a nonprofit partner, brands should also consider certain risks. Before leveraging corporate philanthropy, a firm should make sure the issue they are looking to solve is one that resonates with consumers and shareholders or that the work truly addresses a strategic need of the company. Essentially, using philanthropy without a business strategy behind it can drive performative partnerships rather than truly long-term and impactful ones. In addition, it is important that your firm can use any data tracked by the nonprofit to inform business decisions or impact change. Such data may be used internally—to improve operations or vendor behavior—or externally—to show consumers how their purchasing of your product helps a particular community, for example. But data for data's sake is a waste of everyone's time.

An additional risk to consider is that nonprofit partnership is gener-ally funded by corporate philanthropy and/or investments toward sustainability. Both of these departments often depend on the com-pany staying profitable. As one nonprofit colleague of mine puts it, "Corporate charitable programs are one bad quarter away from being terminated." As you initiate a partnership, both the brand and the nonprofit need to think through ways to sustain the work in case the market turns south. One way to do this, which Nest employs frequently, is to engage multiple brand partners on any new project so the risks and responsibilities get distributed.

Like all partnerships, multilateral ones that bring together multiple partners with differing goals and strategies can be complex. How-ever, we feel that the benefits—and subsequent impacts—can far outweigh these potential risks.

An Example of a Great NGO Partnership: Warby Parker and VisionSpring

One case study of a successful corporate and nonprofit partnership that drives impact is that of Warby Parker and VisionSpring. Warby Parker, started by four students at the Wharton School of Business at the University of Pennsylvania, disrupted the eyeglass market through an innovative approach to providing high-quality, low-cost design alongside a high-tech customer experience.[3] The com-pany also adopted a "buy one, give one" campaign, first launched successfully by Tom's Shoes in the early 2000s. Before joining Wharton, one of the founders, Neil Blumenthal, had served as an executive at VisionSpring, a nonprofit dedicated to addressing vision needs in emerging economies. VisionSpring's philosophy is that it can "reduce poverty and generate opportunity in the devel-oping world through the sale of affordable eyeglasses."[4] The non-profit provides free eye exams and trains local entrepreneurs to start small businesses that sell glasses at an extremely reduced price.

In establishing its model, the NGO knew that if the glasses were provided for free, they would inevitably be discarded, sold, or go unused. By ensuring that there is some level of skin in the game for the recipients of the glasses, they are able to show how productivity and income increases as a result of participation in their program. As Blumenthal intimately knew this model and saw the alignment the organization had with the newly launching Warby Parker, a successful partnership was formed whereby for every pair of glasses sold to an American consumer, the brand would donate both funds to VisionSpring and some pairs of free glasses through targeted VisionSpring projects.* It's difficult to uncouple Warby Parker's success as a brand from the social mission it sold to consumers, and their partnership has led to massive impact. Since the establishment of the partnership, Warby Parker has helped offset the cost of distribution for more than 10 million pairs of glasses through VisionSpring.[5] What I love about this partnership is the symbiotic nature of it. Warby Parker was successful in a large part because they lead with design, customer experience, and price. The social partnership provided an additional storytelling element that, when coupled with solid market strategy, led to astronomical growth and success. And while the brand may focus more heavily on high-design marketing, they unabashedly share the positive results of the partnership. They tell stories of how recipients of the glasses have seen their lives change for the better, show maps of all the countries impacted by the partnership, and provide solid metrics on the economic impact of the new glasses and the numbers of people reached through the partnership. VisionSpring collects these impact metrics and provides them to the Warby Parker team, who then use them to inform their customers. People will buy pairs of Warby Parker glasses time and time again: as a way to support

---

* Technically speaking, it is not primarily a "buy one, give one" model precisely, but is close due to the subsidization of services provided by donations from Warby Parker, and the ease of messaging for the consumer.

the company's social mission but also because the brand offers ever-changing, high-quality designs at reasonable prices. Impactful collaborations come when each partner focuses on their strengths: nonprofits focus on delivering a specific service, and for-profit brands focus on creating a differentiated business model and gaining market share.

We also see exciting nonprofit collaborations that focus on design improvements. Through the organization Cradle to Cradle (C2C),[6] founders Bill McDonough and Michael Braungart have been publicizing the idea of sustainable design for decades. First espoused by Genevieve Reday and Walter Stahel,[7] the concept of a cradle to cradle (aka circular) economy is that products should not be designed to end up in a landfill—aka from "cradle to grave"—but should be reused and recycled for as long as possible. Cradle to Cradle works with companies to show how they can incorporate regenerative design: avoiding harmful chemicals and using as much recycled and recyclable materials as possible. One of my favorite examples of this was the partnership between C2C and the design firm Herman Miller, where the two companies came together to rethink the famous Mirra office chair in the early 2000s. They analyzed every chemical and every production process involved and created a chair that utilized 42% recycled materials and 96% recyclable (reusable) content.[8] The chair received massive critical acclaim and positive customer reaction. Since the relaunch, Herman Miller has continued to refine the production processes and raw materials and in 2013 launched the Mirra 2, increasing the recycled materials content to over 50%.[9] I suspect they are not done yet and will continue to work toward a product that is 100% recyclable. Cradle to Cradle has expanded with the establishment of its own product-certification system and is actively working with countless corporations and governments to further these principles across sectors.

Innovative Collaborations

Nonprofit partnership is not the only way to go; there are countless other collaborative efforts in which brands work with diverse stakeholders, each of whom has different expertise, to drive massive industry change. Two additional examples come from firms who have implemented new supply chain approaches as well as new design techniques that leverage technological innovation in raw materials and production. Brands have learned that they can leverage the creative insights and technologies of newly minted start-up firms to build sustainable solutions to processes or materials. These firms can be nimble, scale fast, and seek outside investment for solution building in ways that large multinational corporations cannot, making their partnership natural and often mutually strategic and impactful.

As the industry looks to improve supply chain innovation, it's important to engage partners to help improve technology, drive innovation, or creatively rethink old practices. One example of a company who is doing all three of these things well is TerraCycle. TerraCycle helps brands and governments recycle and reuse materials. It has established the *Loop* platform as a way to eliminate single-use plastics in consumer goods. Think for a moment about all the plastic bottles and non-recyclable packaging that feels almost unavoidable in your daily purchases: snack-food bags, ice-cream containers, soap and shampoo bottles—the list is endless. The Loop platform[10] provides brands an opportunity and sales channel to pivot to refillable containers for everyday products. It started in 2019 with a milkman-type service program where mail carriers delivered full reusable containers of brand-name products to customers at home. It has since expanded to include online purchasing via Walmart and in-store offerings via Kroger. While the platform is still in its pilot and development phase, TerraCycle is working to eliminate pain points for the consumer such as increasing the places where Loop containers are available or can be brought back for recycling, as well as the diversity of product offerings. This effort requires a lot of collaboration with brands, as the brands need to invest in updating their container designs to accommodate this new sourcing system. For example, how do Loop partners Nutella shift its packaging from plastic to glass, or Nivea shift from single-use plastic containers for razor blades to something more durable? If the pilot proves successful, the platform could support the development of other viable substitutes for traditional single-use packaging, albeit at a price premium for the consumer. If, through their development and scale, Loop can lower their price points so more consumers can afford to participate, the impact could be massive. Loop will need to reach this scale to achieve meaningful sustainability goals. Because Loop packaging is more durable than the average single-use plastic, it requires more energy to make them. However, each time a consumer reuses a Loop container, the average carbon footprint for each use is reduced. Right now, it takes five reuse cycles for a Loop container's footprint per use to match that of a comparable single-use plastic. As more consumers replace single-use plastics with reusable Loop containers, we'll see a greater positive impact from the program.

Building on the success of Cradle to Cradle and the booming interest in circularity, the company Evrnu seeks to tackle waste within the garment industry. The fashion industry is known to be one of the largest polluters on the planet, with 87% of the total fibers used in clothing either ending up in a landfill or incinerator.[11] While recycled polyester has long provided a way to recycle some of this fiber, this only delays the material's inevitable trip to the landfill. Evrnu has established a method to break down fibers (polyester included) to a molecular level and re-spin them into new threads, creating the opportunity to establish an endless cycle of recycled yarn and thereby eliminate waste.[12] Named as one of the best inventions of 2022 by *Time Magazine*, this process shows significant promise. That said, despite exciting collaborations with Stella McCartney, Levi's, and even the oft-criticized fast-fashion brand Zara, it is still very much a start-up. If it is to create system-wide change, it will need to figure out how to scale its technology and how to bring the product to a more accessible price point.

Brand-to-Brand Collaboration

After the Rana Plaza collapse, brands realized that they needed to open paths toward collaboration in order to address unsafe working conditions in factories. At the same time, they realized that they can have a greater and more immediate impact if they collaborate, share costs, and invest strategically. This shift in philosophy has led to some rather unexpected partnerships: brands that would be considered competitors in the market joining forces, sharing knowledge and best practices, and even launching co-branded products all in the name of increased sustainability.

A perfect example of this is the recent collaboration between shoe companies Allbirds and Adidas. Independently, each firm has gained a reputation for their efforts in sustainability. Allbirds, the much newer brand of the two, is known for using natural materials, such as wool, within its shoes and for its commitment to become carbon zero by 2030. (As of this writing, they are on track to reach that goal.) They publish the carbon footprint of each pair of shoes right on the box so that the consumer can know the impact of their purchase. Adidas is a much larger brand but has also been actively pursuing an environmental-impact agenda. They were the first major shoe company to publish a sustainability report and were founding members of initiatives such as Better Cotton and the Fair Labor Association. They have improved their packaging and invested in production techniques to reduce waste, pushing their peer companies and competitors forward. In 2015, Adidas partnered with the nonprofit Parley for the Oceans to create a shoe that used ocean-bound plastics, which are defined as plastics that are either at risk of entering our waterways and oceans or are actively recovered from oceans.

In 2020, Allbirds and Adidas formed a partnership where they would each disclose their learnings on environmentally friendly production and design techniques with one another under the auspices of a shared goal: to create a shoe with zero carbon footprint. The first Futurecraft.Footprint shoe launched as a co-branded effort in 2022, and the companies report that it uses only 2.94 kg of CO_2 per pair.[13] (For comparison, an MIT life cycle assessment estimates that an average pair of running shoes uses more than 13 kg).[14] Both Allbirds and Adidas say that there is much more to come from their work together. Not to be outdone, Nike has also been the leading edge in production innovations. While not partnering directly with other brands, they do open-source their sustainable design playbook at www.nikecirculardesign.com.

Game-Changing Technologies

During our discussion of globalization in Chapter 2, we explored how changing technology accelerated the decentralization of supply chains, from telephones, to faxes and computers, to mobile phones and the Internet. We live in an age in which technology is constantly expanding its role in our everyday lives, where computer science is constantly breaking through the limits of what is possible. I would be remiss if I did not highlight how technology is dramatically changing the ability for brands to have transparency within their supply chains as well.

The first innovative use of technology I want to highlight is a way to increase worker engagement within social compliance. One of the limitations of auditing is that it only provides a snapshot in time. There is no way for someone to monitor conditions and wages every day; the auditor can only see what they can see during the course of their work. But what if you could glean information directly from the workforce on a regular basis? The platform Ulula has figured out a way to do just that.[15] Building off of an idea first implemented by the now-defunct nonprofit LaborVoices, Ulula leverages mobile-phone technology to send brief surveys on behalf of partnering brands to workers via either SMS or voice messaging. The company partners with local mobile-service providers to keep costs as low as possible, and in some cases is able to incentivize workers to respond by offering mobile phone credits. As a result brands can access much more real-time data around topics such as worker treatment, fair pay, and other compliance-related concerns. In addition to the service itself, Ulula analyzes and reports on the findings, feeding the information into their own platforms or existing internal trackers used by their brand partners. In parallel to the surveying, Ulula offers brands the ability to send push notifications directly to workers via SMS or voice messages. This can be really helpful when a brand wants to educate workers on new policies, provide hotlines for them to call if they have issues, and remind them of their roles and responsibilities within the supply chains. This is also extremely important since, on a factory floor with supervisors nearby, it can be challenging for auditors to get accurate or sensitive information from workers. A private, anonymous cell-phone survey can provide richer information and insights as well as challenges directly from the workforce.

The second technology that is shifting the nature of compliance deals with the mapping of the supply chain itself. As we've discussed, as supply chains have become more decentralized, it has become increasingly difficult for brands to know the real flow of raw materials and finished goods as they make their way around the globe. This poses two challenges: firstly, there are concerns around worker well-being. If you do not know who is producing your products or where your raw materials are coming from, how can you ensure that those producers are following your brand code of conduct? Secondly, there is the issue of carbon footprint. How can you determine the environmental sustainability of a supply chain if you cannot accurately calculate how much carbon is produced through the movement of your goods? Another member of *Time Magazine*'s Best Inventions of 2022 list, Sourcemap solves both of these issues by using AI to investigate suppliers with high-risk profiles.[16] It then digitally maps supply chains and shares the information with brand partners so they know the journey their raw materials, components, and finished products make before landing in their warehouses. This enables all of a brand's production nodes to participate in their compliance programs and helps brands determine the most efficient ways to get the products from producer to shelf.

Lastly, blockchain-based solutions are making massive strides in innovation as well. Blockchain is most often associated with cryptocurrencies, such as Bitcoin. And while blockchain is a platform on which cryptocurrency systems can be built, it is also much more. Blockchain is an immutable ledger, where transactions are recorded and stored in blocks (hence "blockchain") and the information is distributed across a particular network, where anyone can view the data. If someone attempts to change the information stored, everyone in the system is notified. In simple terms, blockchain is a cooperative ownership of data (unlike a traditional system where the owner of the platform owns the data). While there is promise in the solutions we will discuss, challenges can also arise in a blockchain-dependent approach if you are not careful. For example, blockchain can be used to build private platforms, in which data is not public, thus making it potentially less transparent than other systems. But the positive possibilities are vast, and two exciting partnerships highlight its potential for use in supply chains.

The first is IBM's work with Walmart to map agriculture supply chains. When Walmart first approached IBM, it was seeking to respond to two very real business challenges: Firstly, when *E. coli* or other outbreaks occur within a particular produce supply chain, the company is forced to eliminate *all* of that particular type of produce for the safety of their customers. This creates a significant amount of waste, has steep financial implications, and, thus, can raise prices. Secondly, the company had faced concerns over the quality of pork in their stores in China, putting their brand reputation at risk. What would it take for the company to be able to instantly identify the provenance of a specific piece of produce or meat? Working with IBM over the course of two years and utilizing the Hyperledger blockchain platform (there are a few different platforms to choose from, some more transparent than others), Walmart was able to reduce the time it took to track the provenance of a particular food item from seven days to just 2.2 seconds![17] The pilot project was a fantastic success, and Walmart and IBM worked to roll out the program more widely throughout their operations. At the last published count, they were able to track 25 different products, and in 2018, Walmart announced that all leafy greens (such as lettuces and spinach) it sold would be tracked on the platform. In addition to mitigating internal risk, this technology could also provide exciting content for consumers. A brand could design QR codes that link directly to stories about the farmers producing the product or information regarding a producer's organic certifications or other sustainable farming practices. I suspect that the consumer—even the price-sensitive ones who compose Walmart's target demographic—would be willing to pay a premium for those products. Or, at the very least, the availability of such information would increase existing consumer loyalty to the brand. Alas Walmart recently announced the program would be paused, I suspect a result of COVID-related market impacts. I cannot imagine it will not be restarted by them or someone else very soon.

The second blockchain application that I want to highlight is the systems-changing work of BanQu, a platform that maps financial transactions all the way down to the end worker, particularly in farming and in waste picking.[18] BanQu was founded on the idea that many individuals and MSMEs (micro and small- to medium-sized enterprises) struggle to access traditional financial systems because they are considered unbankable. They lack credit or business history, operate within the unregulated informal economy, rely on cash-based transactions, and generally pose too much risk for traditional banks to take them on as clients. This lack of oversight has a second negative impact: small farmers or pickers often do not know the going rate for their commodities and therefore rarely get paid the appropriate amount. BanQu provides the ability to accurately track all the transactions that take place within a particular supply chain but also to push information to the last-mile worker so they know what the commodity price should be. They have been able to set up a system that collects, analyzes, and reports complicated data sets to brand partners, while simultaneously sharing the information via simple SMS messages to farmers. As such, even workers who lack Internet access or high-end smartphones can benefit from increased information and communication. BanQu has been recognized as part of the Meaningful Business 100 of 2020 and has partnerships with Coca Cola South Africa to work with bottle collectors, with Anheuser-Busch and Mars for smallholder farmer initiatives, and with many others. They continue to expand their reach, aiming to lift 100 million people out of poverty by 2028.

The Business Case for Innovation

Whether it is through new innovations or partnerships with service providers, every day brings new opportunities for brands to consider. As long as brands stay true to their values and understand their customers and investors, these efforts will yield dividends in one form or another. For some brands, adding partnership and innovation into their business strategy is a new idea and a heavier lift. Others were founded on ideals such as these and act as important North Stars for the market. We will look at two such brands in the next chapter: Patagonia and Unilever.

7

Rays of Sunshine: Stories of Brand Success

"To be successful, you have to have your heart in your business and your business in your heart."
        —*Thomas J. Watson, former Chairman and CEO of IBM*

WHEN DISCUSSING SUSTAINABILITY and impact in business, you often hear two particular brand names come up. The first is Patagonia, the outerwear brand that has earned a reputation for its efforts to reduce the environmental footprint of consumption since its founding. The other is Unilever, one of the largest multinational companies in the world, which was able to incorporate sustainability objectives to great success under the direction of a visionary leader. On paper, Patagonia and Unilever have little in common. Patagonia is a privately held outdoor sporting goods company, while Unilever is a massive conglomerate that produces everything from dish soap to ice cream. But as we will explore in this chapter, both of these companies offer case studies about how businesses can incorporate values-based strategies into their operations while achieving outstanding market success as a result. Let's look at what they have done and how their efforts can be translated to other brands, both large and small.

Patagonia

Patagonia is the perfect example of a brand that has stayed true to its values from day one. Its founder, Yvon Chouinard, is a self-proclaimed "dirt bag," someone who is obsessed with outdoor activities such as mountain climbing and surfing, who works to live rather than lives to work.[1] The company traces its roots back to humble beginnings in the late 1950s when Chouinard started making mountain-climbing equipment and selling it out of the trunk of his car to his friends and other climbing afficionados. After a few short-lived business partnerships, Chouinard established Patagonia as its own brand in 1979 and has been growing the company ever since. As of the writing of this book, it is valued at more than $4.5 billion (even after the COVID market disruptions of 2020–2021).[2] More importantly for the purposes of this book, the brand has always been known for being at the forefront of impact and sustainability, led by Chouinard's vision and passion for protecting the environment. Not afraid to employ strategies that run counter to the traditional profit-first, pro-Friedman philosophy of growing a business, Chouinard founded his business on a number of key principles through which all business decisions flow.

Emphasis on Quality

Patagonia was designed with other "dirt bags" in mind, which means each item of clothing needs to be able to perform in the most grueling conditions of the outdoors. Style is important, but function is essential. As part of the development process, the company uses professional athletes to extensively field-test each product. For the first several decades of the company's existence, Chouinard was actively involved in this testing process, often devoting months to field-test equipment himself. To this day, the company is committed to never cutting corners when it comes to the quality, durability, or performance of its products.[3]

Reduce Environmental Impact

Patagonia is committed to reducing environmental impact wherever and whenever possible, whether in its own production processes and use of raw materials or in encouraging its consumers to purchase less. The company has a five-part philosophy:[4]

1. Lead an examined life;
2. Clean up our own act;

3. Do our penance;

4. Support civil democracy;

5. Influence other companies.

Long before the backlash against fast fashion (the production of low-priced, nearly disposable clothing designed to be worn a few times and then thrown out to encourage increased purchasing), Patagonia was encouraging consumers to buy *fewer* of its products. One of its most famous efforts was a 2011 Black Friday advertisement that stated, "Do Not Buy This Jacket" and featured copy encouraging would-be customers to think twice before purchasing a new garment.[5] Could it be repaired? Could it be reused in some way? Patagonia was the first in its sector to establish a repair, reuse, and recycle program for its clothing. First launched in 2005 as the Patagonia Common Threads Recycling Program, the initiative eventually grew into a much larger operation. Patagonia educates its customers on how to make minor repairs to their jackets and clothing themselves. For more extensive repairs, the company offers in-store and mail-in repair programs. Furthermore, if a customer no longer wants a product, they can trade it in for store credit, and the company will refurbish and resell it on their WornWear platform (which exists both online and in some stores). Patagonia has also teamed up with the Suay Sew Shop organization in order to launch the ReCrafted program, which recycles unusable fabric scraps into brand-new garments.[6] Interestingly, these upcycled clothes are often priced higher than new items, and tend to sell out quickly. The company is truly doing everything it can to ensure its products never end up in a landfill, and data shows that they are slowly but surely creating a circular economy for their sector. Meanwhile, consumers have grown increasingly interested in sustainable fashion. According to the online consignment store ThredUp, the resale market grew 25 times faster than the traditional market in 2019 and is predicted to grow to $64 billion by 2024.[7] Patagonia's efforts are clearly paying off, and most of their large competitors, such as The North Face, have followed on with upcycling programs of their own. If you were a classic private-equity investor, you would probably think this approach is insane; shouldn't for-profit businesses encourage customers to purchase *more* of their items? But Patagonia is willing to sacrifice a certain amount of potential profit in an effort to live by its values—and it trusts that consumers will support those values.

Innovation

Speaking of investments, Patagonia has long been committed to constant innovation, both in terms of environmental sustainability and the durability and performance of its products. Patagonia has its own research laboratory where engineers develop new fabrics and production methods. Through this investment, they have been able to develop innovative approaches, such as utilizing crushed crab shells instead of harmful chemicals to create anti-odor treatments.[8] The company pours millions of dollars into this research every year and is willing to make sacrifices to keep its commitments. For example, after deciding to only use organic cotton in its garments, Patagonia voluntarily reduced the number of styles it offered in order to account for a more limited supply of the raw material. Innovation, for Patagonia, also applies to supply chain development. The company is continually at the forefront of transparency and well-being programs, building and maintaining one of the strictest sets of production protocols in the industry. On their own website, Patagonia outlines their "4-fold approach" when it comes to vetting new potential sourcing partners.[9]

Privately Held

Core to the success of Patagonia's business model is its triple-bottom-line approach to decision making. Unlike in a profit-first firm, where leaders make decisions based solely on the financial bottom line, a triple-bottom-line approach requires them to also consider the environmental and social impacts of their decisions. This can be challenging in public companies where shareholders hold a lot of power and may balk at any strategy that benefits the environment or society at the expense of overall profits. This is further complicated by shareholder turnover. Patagonia's decision to remain privately owned has enabled it to follow a triple-bottom-line business model without having to cater to shareholders. Staying private has also enabled the company's leadership to think creatively about how the company can evolve over time.

Legacy Planning

Recently, Patagonia has made significant headlines through a different kind of innovation: legacy planning. As the Chouinard family planned their exit from the company, they had to decide who would take ownership. Given the company's estimated worth, they could have easily found a buyer, but they didn't want to put the future of the firm into the hands of traditional businesspeople who might abandon the company's commitments. Instead, the family created two entities: The Patagonia Purpose Trust and The Holdfast Collective.[10] The Patagonia Purpose Trust receives all voting stock of the company (2% of all the shares) and is designed to ensure the firm never deviates from its values. The remaining 98% of the shares, all the non-voting stock, will be held by the Holdfast Collective. All profits from these shares that are not reinvested back into Patagonia will be distributed annually in the form of grants toward efforts to fight climate change. Through this highly unusual structure, Chouinard and Patagonia are saying two things. One, that no one—not even the founder of a wildly successful and beloved company—needs billions upon billions of dollars; enough is enough. Chouinard has accumulated an estimated $1.2 billion because of Patagonia's success. Why continue to accumulate wealth when you can use your influence to effect meaningful change on the world? Second, the Chouinards are committing to the statement they made in the press when they announced the action: that the Earth is Patagonia's only shareholder. It will be *very* interesting to see how this action influences other companies in the future, particularly start-ups and social enterprises that reach the point of founder exit.

How Patagonia Makes It Work

So how can other companies translate Patagonia's approach to their own efforts at sustainability? There are a few key factors at play.

Decision Making

As outlined in Chapter 3, the Patagonia team firmly takes an *integrated* approach when it comes to corporate social responsibility and the responsible sourcing team. Conversations around business strategy *start* with environmental and social impacts; they are not simply a by-product or bonus of another strategy. As an example, Patagonia was one of the first brands to join Nest's Steering Committee in 2014, working on the launch of our Ethical Handcraft Program. Despite their early involvement, it took several years before we formally launched our product-based initiative with the brand. This is not because the brand did not see the value in handcraft or artisanal products but because the company had to go through many layers of decision making before it could adopt this new opportunity. In parallel with the product-design itself, any new material or production partner needed to meet Patagonia's high environmental standards, followed by their high standards for social compliance. At any point along the way, if the team was unable to get the answers they were looking for, or help co-create solutions to address their concerns, they had the ability to push pause on the project until a new opportunity or solution presented itself. In a world where production deadlines and delivery often outweigh all other concerns, it was refreshing to see this kind of trust and authority placed on the Patagonia team. And it truly felt like a team effort, with design and sourcing walking hand-in-hand with the compliance and CSR team instead of being at odds with one another. In 2021, after beginning our work together in 2017, it was thrilling for us at Nest to see Patagonia announce its collection of handcrafted indigo-dyed Khadi fabrics from India through a Nest partnership.[11] In addition to offering a new product to Patagonia customers, the effort allowed the company to support an ancient craft tradition (previously popularized by Mahatma Gandhi) and support a rural community of artisans in the process.

Corporate Culture

Another factor to Patagonia's success is its strong corporate culture, which has led to an extremely loyal employee base. The company strives to always prioritize the health and happiness of its employees. Everyone who works at Patagonia is there because they firmly believe in the mission and share a passion for the outdoors. As Chouinard famously once stated, "You can teach a dirtbag how to do business, but [you] can't teach an MBA graduate how to climb."[12] He purposefully hired people who shared his worldview.

Surf conditions are posted on the wall at the brand headquarters in Ventura, California, and it is not uncommon for employees to cancel meetings if the swells are up.[13] As an homage to that ideal, Chouinard even titled his book *Let My People Go Surfing,* and the company encourages employees to take paid sabbaticals to explore nature and volunteer for social or environmental NGOs. I think part of his employees' loyalty is inspired by Chouinard's leadership style. He is a true visionary, but he also knows his limits. He does not run the day-to-day business operations and hasn't really served that role since the founding of the company. He jokes that his strategy is a different kind of MBA: Management by Absence.[14]

This loyalty was tested a bit during the COVID-19 pandemic, when for the first time the firm had to put people on furlough. It was one of the first retail companies to close all its brick-and-mortar stores because of the pandemic.[15] Shortly thereafter it went through a sudden leadership transition when CEO Rose Marcario abruptly stepped down in June 2020.[16] But the company has been able to weather that storm, under the leadership of longtime Patagonia employee and now CEO Ryan Gellert.

Customer Loyalty

In addition to strong employee loyalty, Patagonia has an extremely loyal customer base. Patagonia makes a premium product. Thanks to its quality, durability, innovation, and reputation, it can charge 20% more than its competitors for comparable products. That customer loyalty also means that Patagonia needs to spend very little (less than 1% of its budget) on direct marketing. Instead, Patagonia invests a great deal in raising awareness of environmental issues through its publications and videography efforts, such as the Footprint Chronicles, which share how customers use their products.

The only time they pay for advertising (outside of efforts like the "Do Not Buy This Jacket" campaign) is to raise awareness of new-store openings or in-store events and gatherings. They envision their stores to be more like community centers, where like-minded people can gather, get educated, and commit to action in support of the environment. This also underscores that less can be more: when the message being shared by a company is consistent and steadfast, the company does not need to shout as loudly.

Freedom of Decision Making

Finally, I think it is important to return quickly to Patagonia's ownership structure. The company's private ownership has facilitated its ability to take risks. Because it does not answer to shareholders, the company can make decisions in line with its values, even if it comes at the expense of profits. In addition, Patagonia has been free to visibly support divisive issues such as abortion rights without concern of shareholder reaction. And, as a brand it can publicly shame Wall Street firms for pursuing business strategies that run counter to its values. For example, in 2019, the company announced it would no longer sell its fleece vests to financial firms through its corporate marketing program.[17] Knowing that these vests had become extremely popular among a certain cohort of Wall Street types, this move demonstrated that Patagonia is willing to actively reduce its own profits in order to sever its association with an industry they find harmful.

Some Challenges with the Patagonia Model

While Patagonia's business model has led to tremendous impact, it is also a model that is not easily replicated.

Circularity versus Production

Firstly, there is an inherent tension between the desire to reduce negative environmental impacts and the need for a brand to grow. If a brand's goal is to establish a fully circular system of clothing, then, eventually, it would have to stop producing any new product. While Patagonia's upcycled clothing does sell for a higher price point, I cannot imagine that those sales alone would be enough to sustain the brand long term. Will Patagonia then cease to exist? At some point, does Patagonia transition to a nonprofit that exists to combat climate change through reuse versus a brand whose profits support that effort? Any other brand that is looking to establish itself needs to wrestle with this tension, perhaps even earlier than Patagonia did in its development. Patagonia was able to establish its upcycling program after amassing a loyal customer base willing to spend a premium, something that takes other companies years to establish, if ever. Within larger companies, the conversation around circularity is often siloed given the conflict with the corporation's main mission of producing new goods.

Corporate Size and Organizational Structure

While we will delve into the case study of Unilever as a multinational brand tackling ambitious social responsibility goals, both size and organization structure are two critical considerations when discussing how a brand can approach social impact. Patagonia's relatively small size and narrow focus on outerwear and an outdoor lifestyle allow it to be very focused on tackling aggressive goals. These goals become much more complicated at companies with more diverse, or scaled, production. Commitments to more expensive materials, or more scarce materials (such as organic cotton) can be next to impossible when discussed at massive scale or with a low target price point. The private holding of Patagonia, as discussed, also allows for easier decision making.

Consumer Reach

Speaking of price points, another challenge to consider is that Patagonia's high-end status means that its products are out of reach for the majority of consumers. Patagonia can only engage in systems change by convincing upper-middle class consumers to change their purchasing habits, and to use those profits to combat climate change. Does most of the population, then, have to stick with fast fashion? One critique of sustainability movements is their lack of democratization; very few models truly uphold the principles of social responsibility at a low price point. This means companies and consumers have to make difficult choices. Deeper innovation by companies committed to producing lower-cost items could yield future results, but for now, scalability remains a challenge.

Unexpected Events

When a brand is so firmly basing its reputation on the health and welfare of its employees, what happens when unexpected events, such as COVID-19, occur? Patagonia's current CEO has acknowledged how difficult it has been for the company to work through the employee furloughs and challenges of 2020–21.[18] Only time will tell if this decision results in a negative long-term impact on the company culture or if remaining and future employees will stay loyal to the brand. For all companies and managers, there will always be a fine line between being a supervisor and being a supporter and friend. Each company needs to decide for itself where that line sits.

Unilever

We now move from the niche and highly successful work of Patagonia to the massive efforts of Unilever. Unlike the small and privately held corporate structure of Patagonia, as of 2023, Unilever is made up of hundreds of brands, each operating its own line of business across 190 countries.[19] While Patagonia focuses exclusively on outdoor sportswear, Unilever sells products across almost every consumer-packaged goods (CPG) category you can imagine. Unilever is a goliath, with a current valuation of more than $126 billion.[20] (Patagonia, by contrast, is worth just over $4 billion.) It is also a much more established firm, tracing its roots all the way back to the late 1800s. In comparison, Patagonia feels like a young upstart. But there are two aspects of the Unilever story that mirror that of Patagonia's: it too was founded with purpose in mind, having virtually coined the phrase "doing well by doing good,"[21] and its turnaround story is firmly rooted in the values of environmental sustainability and the leadership of a visionary CEO.

When Paul Polman took the helm of Unilever as CEO in 2009, the company was in serious trouble. In the midst of a global economic downturn, Unilever's growth through acquisition was slowing. The firm was losing market share to its competitors, having been passed in size by Procter & Gamble, and had experienced revenue loss or stagnation for more years than not during the early 2000s.[22] Unlike Chouinard, Polman was a seasoned businessman, an industry insider who had previously been an executive at both Procter & Gamble and Nestlé during his 30-plus year career. Given Polman's extensive corporate background, one might have expected him to pull the traditional levers of corporate turnaround during a period of crisis: large-scale layoffs of staff or the selling of underperforming brands. Instead, he took a revolutionary approach that has since become a case study in effective leadership, change management, and, yes, corporate responsibility.

Polman's Vision: The Unilever Sustainable Living Plan

In 2010, in the midst of Unilever's troubling performance, Polman announced a major initiative, the Unilever Sustainable Living Plan (USLP).[23] Through this plan, the company would return to its purpose-driven values and strive to double the size of its business while reducing its environmental footprint and increasing social impact at the same time.[24] By 2020, Unilever was going to:

- Improve health and well-being for more than one billion people;
- Reduce environmental impact by one-half;
- Enhance the livelihoods of millions of people.

What's more, Polman declared that Unilever would target emerging economies as the source of 80% of its growth.[25] As a result of this announcement, Polman was met with more than a few raised eyebrows, both from employees and shareholders. How in the world was he going to pull this off?

Polman and the USLP team broke down these broad goals into seven key objectives and more than 50 measurable targets across the company. Over the next 10 years, the Unilever Sustainable Living Plan became a massive success. The company was able to motivate its more than 165,000 employees and millions of supply chain workers to strive toward a common goal. At the same time, it was able to deliver on its growth objectives. Over the course of Polman's tenure, the firm generated a 290% shareholder return and once again became a dominant force in the market, outperforming major competitors.[26] The brands within its portfolio the company had identified as "sustainable living brands" (those with a stated goal of sustainability) grew twice as fast as the rest of the brand portfolio and drove half of Unilever's overall growth. Investors were thrilled, Polman was praised for his ambitious leadership, and the employees were happy, reporting 15% higher job-satisfaction numbers than they had in 2009.[27]

The Ingredients of Unilever's Success

What Unilever accomplished is certainly worthy of praise, but *how* they accomplished this effort is why they are discussed in the halls of so many business schools and used as the gold standard in corporate social responsibility circles. Let's take a look at the key reasons Polman and Unilever were able to navigate this pivot into greater sustainability so successfully (while also turning around a company that was financially in trouble to boot).

Leadership

Without a doubt, Polman proved himself to be an exemplary leader. While much of his success was external (he was not afraid to speak his truth and seek to bring other firms and sectors along in his crusade to change the nature of business), it was his internal leadership that led to the greatest impact. Within Unilever, he was able to: (a) develop a clear vision, (b) employ tactics to energize the workforce through goal setting, benchmarking, and communicating, (c) empower leaders and employees to create change and innovation on their own, and, finally, (d) know when and how to make an exit from the company (Polman stepped down as CEO in 2019) so that the firm did not solely rely on his vision to continue to innovate and succeed.

Beyond Polman himself, the rest of Unilever's executive team played a critical role in the USLP's success. Polman knew he had to surround himself with like-minded believers or the initiative would fail. Within his first few years at the company, almost one-third of the top 100 executives had been replaced. In addition, Polman created room in the C-suite for leadership specifically around sustainability. He transitioned the chief marketing officer position into a role that bridged both communications and sustainability and eventually created a new chief sustainability officer role that reported into this CMO. At the time, the role of a chief sustainability officer was still relatively new. DuPont (the chemical company) created the first CSO role in 2004, but by 2010 less than 20 large firms had appointed people to this position.[28] This move signaled to the whole firm that sustainability now had a seat at the leadership table and was not just an activity done off to the side. Taking a play from Patagonia's handbook, Polman embedded sustainability into the company's core business strategy and operations.

Goals, Objectives, and Measurable Outcomes

It is one thing for a CEO to make broad declarations, but how could these turn into action? Polman did this through the incorporation of strategic objectives and measurable outcomes that everyone would be tracking toward. The three goals of improving health and well-being, halving the environmental impact, and enhancing livelihoods were translated into seven core pillars around health and hygiene, nutrition, greenhouse gases, water use, waste, sustainable sourcing, and better livelihoods. In turn, these pillars got translated into more than 50 measurable outcomes, where firm data could be collected and analyzed in order to determine performance.[29] In one sense, Unilever got a little lucky in that, in 2006, before the launch of USLP, it had already started collecting some sustainability indicators for each of its brands. Instead of building a data strategy from scratch, therefore, they could build upon their existing one. In such a complicated initiative, it is important for employees to have enough feedback so they can understand if their actions and efforts are having a positive impact toward reaching goals. Benchmarking across the organization helped brands see where they were excelling and where they may be lagging behind so each team could decide how to devote resources appropriately.

Communication, Communication, Communication

The transition of the CMO role was done very purposefully, as communication was a key component of the USLP game plan. Externally, executives at Unilever made their commitments extremely public. They reported out their objectives but also their progress. They took the stage at industry events and claimed a leadership role in the United Nations Sustainable Development Goals and at the Davos World Economic Forum. Perhaps most importantly, they also communicated their belief that the nature of business as a whole had to change, not only for the success of Unilever but for the sake of the planet as well. Polman ruffled many Wall Street feathers by proclaiming that the short-term thinking of investors was partially to blame. Unilever would no longer issue quarterly earnings reports beyond what was required by law. He famously stated, "We need to know why we are here [at Unilever]. The answer is, for consumers, not shareholders. If we are in sync with consumer needs and the environment in which we operate, and take responsibility for society as well as our employees, then the shareholder will also be rewarded."[30] Remember Friedman? In his way, Polman was saying that corporate responsibility was not an impediment to shareholder value but a key driver of it.

Given the complexity of the Unilever corporation (with its more than 165,000 employees globally) and of the USLP task at hand, internal communication strategies were just as important as external ones. Upon the rollout of the plan, executives hosted company forums and team meetings, making in-person site visits to various points of production as well. Each team understood which of the identified targets their brand was going to focus on, as well as how they were performing to those goals more generally.

Finally, given that Unilever's environmental objectives revolved around both the production of and the *use* of their products, the company needed to make sure their customers supported the effort. Brand marketing teams engaged in internal workshops to understand how their brand connected to the USLP objectives, as well as how the brand could be positioned with the consumer in order to help change consumer behavior. A few creative examples of this include the Persil laundry detergent "Dirt Is Good" advertising campaign,[31] which encouraged parents to let their children play outside to support their development. Another brand, Suave, included discounts on low-flow shower heads with the purchase of its shampoos to encourage water conservation in the United States.[32] We will discuss some of the challenges Unilever faced momentarily, but in looking at their overall effort it is clear that in the areas where Unilever fell short of its objectives, consumers' resistance to changing their behavior takes much of the blame.

Learning from Successes

In addition to having individual brands track their performance and hold themselves to established company-wide benchmarks, the firm as a whole was able to identify the leaders and the laggards regarding each objective. Where things were going well, the company would lean in and work to understand what that brand was doing to promote success. The company would then share this information across the organization so that everyone could benefit. Furthermore, the company took the extra time needed to work with the management teams of brands that were falling behind, providing them additional support and resources so that they could keep working toward their goals.

Additionally, the identification of the Sustainable Living Brands feels like a stroke of genius. In any large change-management effort, it is important to have some sort of rallying cry or point of inspiration. Out of the 30 core brands in the Unilever portfolio, 11 embodied the ideals of the USLP, were already outperforming the others, and helped the company demonstrate that it did not need to start everything from scratch to meet its goals. On top of highlighting this group of brands, Polman declared a goal to make Unilever the world's largest certified B Corp. Some brands within the Sustainable Living portfolio had already achieved B Corp status, and beloved ice-cream brand Ben and Jerry's became certified in 2012, the same year it was acquired by Unilever. Unilever officially became B Corp certified in 2022, and, as of this writing, eight of the Sustainable Living have achieved that certification.

In short, the success of the USLP effort proves that companies can, indeed, do well by doing good. When reflecting on the first 10 years of the USLP,[33] Unilever was able to report major progress on the three top-level goals, highlighting some of their achievements:

- Reached 1.3 billion people through health and hygiene programs;
- Reduced the total waste footprint per consumer use of products (meaning the footprint of waste from production through consumption) by 32%, achieving zero waste to landfill across all factories;
- Reduced greenhouse gas emissions in manufacturing by 65% and achieved 100% renewable grid electricity across all production sites;
- Enabled 2.34 million women in the Unilever supply chain to access programs on safety, skill development, or expansion of work opportunities, and created a gender-balanced workplace (internally and in contracted facilities) with 51% of management roles being held by women.

Targeting Emerging Economies for Growth

Why did Unilever target emerging economies for 80% of its growth? Most likely because, in developed areas such as the United States and Europe, the consumer base was already fairly saturated. In places like this, Unilever could only gain market share by stealing it from one of their direct competitors. By contrast, in other parts of the world, millions of people were not yet using the types of detergents or cleaners (or other offerings) that a company like Unilever could provide. Here they needed to convince the market of the value of their company and their products—a much lighter lift than convincing existing users of such products to switch brands. The strategy is similar to what other brands, such as Mastercard, have done with great success. In Mastercard's case, the credit-card giant established its Center for Inclusive Growth,[34] which focuses philanthropic efforts on improving access to financial services for the billions of people around the world who have traditionally lacked access to banks and the capital they provide. While Mastercard's work is extremely altruistic in nature, they are also able to cultivate new potential clients through this initiative.

Not All Sunshine and Rainbows

While the progress made by Unilever in their initial USLP was phenomenal, they have struggled in a few places, and the company has faced challenges since Polman's departure.[35] So that others could learn from them, Unilever was very open about the places where it did not meet its objectives. Firstly, it missed some of its targets around water use after acquiring a new shampoo company that necessarily increased the firm's water use (the company factors in how much water consumers must use alongside their products when calculating their sustainability metrics). Additionally, try as they might, the company had very little success convincing consumers to reduce their water usage by taking shorter showers, washing clothes with cold water only, or using dry shampoos. There were also areas where Unilever quickly realized that they alone could not solve a systemic challenge. As a result, they became a leading force for many industry coalitions, including those focused on reducing deforestation within palm-oil supply chains and addressing sanitation issues in Southeast Asia.

Additionally, one of the biggest sources of strain on any organization is a leadership transition. Could Polman have stayed on at Unilever for another decade or more? Of course. But both he and the firm were better served with his departure. Polman now runs his own organization, called IMAGINE, which helps other CEOs and leaders embed sustainability thinking into their organizations. He handed the reigns of Unilever over to Alan Jope, who certainly has big shoes to fill, especially given the impact of COVID-19. As with every other firm on the planet, COVID put Unilever's plans on hold while it pivoted to respond to the crisis. But due to its focus on innovation and sustainable solutions over the last decade, Unilever feels uniquely prepared to bend and sway with the new reality of a post-pandemic landscape.

Next Steps

With any successful initiative, the question becomes what happens after the stated goals are met or the timeline for execution has lapsed. In most cases, this presents the opportunity for creating a new strategic vision leveraging the learnings—both good and bad—from previous efforts. This was true in the case of Unilever as well. The USLP lives on and continues to iterate new solutions. The company unveiled the second phase of the initiative in 2020. It incorporates feedback from tens of thousands of Unilever employees, and the company continues to transparently communicate about its work by providing progress reports to the public via its corporate website.

Patagonia and Unilever Are Not Alone

Patagonia and Unilever are just two examples of firms that I (and many others) feel are doing it right. There are countless other firms that are doing new and exciting things to promote sustainability and social impact, and odds are there is one in your industry that is worth paying attention to. Maybe its Tony's Chocolonely, which is trying to combat slave labor in the chocolate supply chain by rethinking their approach to dealing with independent farmers (and selling delicious chocolate bars in the process). Or perhaps its Fairphone, which is showing how a smartphone company can move away from planned obsolescence and ensure that the rare minerals involved in smartphone production are mined responsibly. Or perhaps you are thinking of the next innovative idea. No matter what the circumstance, the lessons learned from both Patagonia and Unilever will help inform the next generation of successful impact-based businesses and consumers. Embedded in all this hard work is how the goals and results are communicated to the public and leveraged for competitive advantage. That question brings us to the next chapter: how to tell an accurate story about your impact efforts and avoid the pitfalls of greenwashing.

8

Let Me Tell You a Story: The Responsible Marketing of Responsible Sourcing

"The most powerful person in the world is the storyteller. The storyteller sets the vision, values, and agenda of an entire generation that is to come."

— Steve Jobs

WITH CONSUMER SUPPORT at stake and brands fighting each other tooth and nail for a space in the market, corporations are leveraging their sustainability practices, including responsible sourcing, to change the way they present themselves to their audience. James Walker, Executive Vice President and General Manager of the Baltimore office of global public relations agency Weber Shandwick, confirms:

> The communications industry has noted the rise of the ethical consumer for quite some time, and this shift in consumer expectations has been a net positive because it has provided senior communications leaders a seat at the decision-making table. In recent years, strategic communications leaders have been able to demonstrate the value of thoughtful brand-level communications, married with strong responses to ongoing social issues and reputation management. Good public relations practitioners have saved brands and businesses at large, and giving communications teams more authority in the creation of authentic messaging around impact has prevented several organizations from being in the hot seat to begin with.

In other words, just as we saw with Polman's strategy at Unilever, communications play a critical role in determining the success of your responsible-sourcing initiatives since, ultimately, sales must follow suit. If a firm can successfully implement responsible-sourcing practices *and* engage their consumers on that work, your ability to magnify your impact significantly increases. You live, and die, by your reputation.

Let's start our conversation about how to message your sustainability initiatives effectively with a short marketing and communications primer. In this chapter I am referencing two different but related activities: one is product-specific branding and marketing, and the other is related to business-wide messaging—communicating your value proposition and mission as a brand overall.

The Basics of Product Marketing and Brand Value Messaging

In case you do not come from a marketing background, the general principle of product marketing revolves around the four Ps: product, price, placement, and promotion.

- **Product:** What type of product you are offering and trying to sell? This could be a physical object or a service you provide. What attributes does it possess that would be of interest to the consumer you are trying to coax into making a purchase?
- **Price:** Compared to similar items from your competitors, how do you want to price your product? How does that price relate to your value proposition, and how is it related to the quality of components or ingredients you use in making your product? Is it organic? Is it a luxury good?
- **Placement:** Where is the product physically placed? In a grocery store, it could be what shelf or aisle houses your item. Or does it live in a special end-of-aisle display to bring more attention to what you are trying to sell? What channel(s) should you utilize (a physical location, e-commerce)?
- **Promotion:** This includes all of the advertising and public relations you are utilizing to convince people to buy your product. Social-media campaigns, print ads, hangtang messaging, in-store signage, web advertisements, and influencer marketing are perhaps the most common strategies.

Messaging around overall brand value, mission, and story can leverage some of the above strategies, particularly promotion, but also includes public-facing messages intended to raise overall awareness of the company rather than a specific product. In addition, brands may launch campaigns that highlight causes or issues that are linked to their company values as a way to promote more public awareness and dialogue and to communicate their values to their target customers.

In both product-specific and overall-awareness efforts, brands are looking to leverage the rise in consumer interest around sustainability through several different types of marketing. As we will explore in this chapter, increasingly, businesses are launching advertising campaigns to express their commitment to environmental and social issues. Research from New York University's Center for Sustainable Business shows us how companies are addressing this rise of consumer interest in their branding and marketing efforts. As of 2021, sustainably marketed products (ones that have some sort of impact-based labeling) reached 17% of the overall market share of consumer-packaged goods, up from 13.7% just a few years earlier in 2015. This represents a growth rate 2.7 times faster than that of conventionally marketed products.[1] Secondly, the industry-wide initiatives we discussed in Chapter 5 often have very public commitments, and brands declare their overall impact objectives by participating in those efforts. For example, in June 2020, Amazon pledged $2 billion to the Climate Pledge in support of efforts that will decarbonize the earth.[2] Another example is the commitments from companies as wide-ranging as Macy's to Sephora to the 15% pledge—an initiative that encourages companies to commit to sourcing 15% of their total product from Black-owned producers.[3]

But what happens when these branding or advertising campaigns and/or social media efforts to promote dialogue around issues are poorly received and the company faces backlash instead of achieving its marketing goals? In this ever-changing landscape of consumer interest, brands are still figuring out the right approach, and the consumer is increasingly more skeptical. A 2021 Nielsen survey found that 55% of respondents were not convinced that brands were working on true progress in addressing societal issues.[4] An example of this is the fashion brand Everlane, the fashion start-up who trademarked the term "Radical Transparency." After making bold claims on how they were approaching responsibility in new and bold ways, they came under fire for a variety of issues, including a toxic working culture characterized by anti-Black sentiment as well as a lack of accountability to back up their aggressive responsible-sourcing claims. Their messaging did not line up with their behavior, and the company was eviscerated in the press as well as by their consumers on social media. Sustainability expert Luke Smitham was quoted in the *New York Times* as saying, "They [Everlane] do some good work, but I wouldn't describe it as radical. The most radical thing about Everlane is the marketing."[5] This was a particularly brutal criticism, given that Everlane was seen at the time as the poster child for the rising movement of sustainable start-ups that were going to disrupt the fashion industry. Even now in 2023, while Everlane has made strides to try and right the ship, consumers and industry observers treat any support of social issues by the firm with distrust and skepticism.[6]

Given the opportunity to differentiate from firm competition through sustainability initiatives and the negative consequences if brand messaging is received poorly, it is important to know how to communicate an impact-narrative effectively. This marketing road map will look very different for each brand and will depend on the values and goals of the firm. Also, given the business opportunities created by impact-related activities, brands need to avoid the temptation to communicate a false message—a process known as "greenwashing" or "woke washing." In this chapter, we will look at how brands can effectively communicate their legitimate hard work without succumbing to greenwashing, consciously or not.

Impact Natives versus Impact Immigrants

Communicating about impact, or taking a stand on a societal issue related to your supply chain or business, can be a fraught exercise: you will never please everyone and will most definitely anger and alienate some of your stakeholders. This may be the result of imperfect messaging, or simply because not everyone is going to buy in to your decisions, especially if they involve controversial subjects. Why are some brands celebrated when they communicate their efforts while others get slammed for being inauthentic or performative every time they stick their neck out in support of a cause?

The first factor to consider here is a concept highlighted in a 2017 article titled "Competing on Social Purpose."[7] The authors of the article introduce the idea of social purpose natives versus social purpose immigrants. Native brands have impact baked into their business right from their founding. Think again about Patagonia or Warby Parker. These companies were founded with a specific mission that continues to direct their business strategy—how they source products, how they build margin and profit into their value proposition to their consumer, what they do with the proceeds of those product sales, etc. When Patagonia creates an advertising campaign (like their powerful "We're all screwed" video from 2020 that urges individual consumers to actively work toward addressing climate change),[8] consumers receive the message much more positively than they would a similar campaign by, say, ExxonMobil, which has a long track record of environmentally extractive processes.

One of the earliest and most well-known examples of greenwashing was a television advertisement put out by the oil company Chevron in the mid-1980s.[9] It depicted beautiful scenes of nature, including a mother bear running in green fields with her cubs, indicating that Chevron was hard at work deep underground while that bear family hibernated for the winter. The video implied that Chevron's work drilling oil actually benefited nature and the environment. The public received the ad poorly, and marketers still talk about the company's misstep 30 years later. In fact, in 2022 comedian, screenwriter, and producer Adam McKay made a vicious satirical (and not-safe-for-work) reboot of the ad,[10] which went viral, getting over four million views within the first week it was posted. Consumers look favorably on social-purpose narratives from Patagonia because the company is a social-purpose native. Chevron, meanwhile, is an immigrant, and the public will, understandably, view any effort they make to bake sustainability into their story with skepticism.

Being an impact native brand does not always give a company a pass, however. Consider the Everlane example. They were built on social-responsibility principles and had built a fast-growing and loyal consumer base. They struggled for two reasons: they did not have quantifiable proof points to show that their commitments were being executed and, worse, had public examples that contradicted earlier sentiments. Being deemed a native brand requires both public commitments and a track record of provable success.

Despite the challenges non-native brands face, we do need them to make strategic pivots if we want to live in a more sustainable world. Marketing to consumers and investors helps support these efforts, so brands need to feel confident in their messaging and the ability to move in new directions. Think about Polman at Unilever: the brand was struggling financially and had not made significant public commitments around corporate responsibility. He was an ambitious leader, and part of his ambition included creating a *new* vision of sustainability for the brand. This required both internal and external communications and consumer buy-in on the new direction. How can an impact immigrant do this and succeed?

First, the brand will need to identify the societal tensions that most affect their consumers and/or investors, particularly the tensions that are most closely related to the brand's legacy or heritage. For example, let's look at the pilot program between EVRNU and Zara, which was highlighted in Chapter 6. In announcing this partnership, Zara, which is known as a "fast-fashion" brand that produces mass quantities of cheap, essentially disposable garments, did not pretend it was going to change its entire business model and reduce the number of styles it produces. Nor did the brand imply that its overall business is good for the environment. Instead, it used its collaboration with EVRNU to signal how it is working to source raw materials more responsibly.

A second factor to consider for both impact immigrants and impact natives is the authenticity of the message and the work. Simply put, what actions stand behind the marketing message? Is there a partnership with a respected implementing organization? How specific is the brand being about the problem they are looking to tackle or issue they are looking to highlight for their consumer? With Zara, the brand wants to reduce the use of plastics and the overall amount of waste produced by the fashion industry. I briefly referred to an impact native example of authenticity at the end of Chapter 3 with Nisolo, a shoe company founded on the idea of artisan-crafted, ethically made shoes. Nisolo has been extremely vocal about their responsible-sourcing journey, publicly sharing both the positive developments and the challenges they've faced. For example, while looking deeper into their supply chain, they discovered that workers at some of the factories from which they sourced were not earning a living wage. Instead of focusing its messaging only on the positive stories, Nisolo took their consumers along with them. As part of their journey, the company determined appropriate wages for their workers and helped to establish the #LowestWageChallenge,[11] which calls on all brands to move beyond a minimum-wage requirement in favor of a living-wage one and provides a road map to do so—including transparently sharing the wages of even their lowest paid in the supply chain.

Greenwashing can also impact a brand in ways beyond consumer reaction. As I indicated in Chapter 6, potential partnering organizations look at a brand's track record of authenticity. At Nest, we carefully analyze each potential new partner that expresses interest in our program, as the last thing we want is to enable marketing campaigns that do not have teeth, longevity, or sustainable commitments behind the work. We look at what they have done in the past, as well as the scope of what they are committing to do in the partnership. Additionally, we consider how and what they have communicated about their sustainability efforts. Did they use their communication strategy to speak genuinely about the specific actions they took? Or did they use it to try and improve the overall brand image without providing details or metrics on the impact they've had? One litmus test we often use is to consider how our ultimate stakeholder—the craft worker—would perceive their effort and communication. What would Laurie, the basket weaver in the Philippines, think if she saw the article or ad campaign announcing the project?

Marketing Impact: Key Considerations

Both purpose natives and purpose immigrants need a clear road map to determine the marketing strategy to promote your responsibly sourced product or awareness of your brand's sustainability. By carefully planning, you can hopefully avoid some of the more common missteps. Before you communicate about your sustainability efforts, you need to make some key decisions.

Decision #1: When

The timing of your communications will certainly vary depending on what type of news you have to share or announcement you have to make. If your firm has joined an industry initiative and is publicly announcing its goals to reach new milestones in sustainability and impact through that initiative, you do not need to have everything figured out when you go to press. Think about Polman's approach to the Unilever Sustainable Living Plan. However, if you are marketing a specific product with specific traits that you emphasize as environmentally friendly or high impact, you need to have developed and tested the product in order to make verifiable claims.

Decision #2: How

When you are ready to share your news and messaging with your stakeholders, you will have to think about *how* to position your message in relation to your overall brand story. Do you want to lead with purpose over profit and make your efforts the leading story of your company? Or do you want to use it to support other key characteristics of your brand that would attract consumers—such as convenience, quality, or design? Think back to the Warby Parker marketing strategy. Even though the company has always prioritized helping underfunded communities gain access to affordable eyewear, it does not position itself as a social business or nonprofit but instead an eyewear company committed to great design and affordable prices (with an added social benefit). This is a strategic decision.

While leading with sustainability can help distinguish a brand from its competitors, it does not guarantee an increase in market share. While most consumers are increasingly focused on minimizing the negative impact of their purchases, many are unwilling to sacrifice quality or convenience to do so. A Getty Images research report from 2020 showed that, out of 10,000 people surveyed globally, 92% paid attention to environmental issues because they believed the way we treat our planet will have a large impact on the future.[12] Still, a whopping 48% said that, while they knew they should change their purchasing habits to positively impact the environment, they are not willing to switch to an inferior or less convenient product to do so. Warby Parker seemed to know what it was doing by putting its business first!

To use another example, one of my former students works for Nespresso, a firm known for their innovations in both technology and sustainability in the coffee industry. He told me that one of the company's biggest ongoing challenges is convincing customers to recycle their espresso pods. The company does everything it can to make the process of recycling them easy, even providing the postage-paid return packaging with every new order of coffee they deliver. However, they find that their customer often wants some sort of additional reward for the act of diverting these pods from the landfill. It turns out that, even with its mostly frictionless recycling program, Nespresso reports that only 29% of its used pods get recycled.[13] For Nespresso to successfully bring its full impact story to fruition, it will need to figure out how to successfully convince its consumers to actively participate in the recycling program.

Of course, not all consumers need an additional reward to encourage sustainable behavior. As we demonstrated earlier in this book, a growing number of consumers are interested in purchasing second-hand or upcycled clothing; some are even willing to pay a premium to do so. But the *majority* still needs to see additional benefits (or, at least, not have to sacrifice quality or convenience) to shift their purchasing behavior. This is why you need to be careful about *how* you tell your story. Can you clearly demonstrate how your customer can partner with you to increase positive impacts? Or how purchasing your product instead of more conventional items will reduce negative impacts? Or how by supporting your brand, your customer is joining a larger movement to make a more equitable society?

Decision #3: Who

You also need to decide *who* you want to be communicating your progress with. This will determine not only the best messaging but also the best channel through which to share it, since the avenues for consumers versus investors look very different and require different strategies. In terms of consumers, you have quite a few tactics to choose from. Is it through hangtags, with their very small space for verbiage? What about in-store signage? In 2013, shortly after West Elm made a significant commitment to source handmade product at the Clinton Global Initiative, beautiful, large-scale posters that told the stories and shared photos of the people behind these products started appearing in their stores. When Nest established a partnership with FEED and American Eagle to sell handmade bags from Guatemala, the images of the weaving community appeared on electronic billboards in Times Square. An increasing opportunity for consumers comes in the form of QR codes, which gives consumers the ability to access significant information via the Internet—videos, longer format stories, blogs, and more—about a specific product while allowing the brand to update the information in real time. We are already getting to a point where brands can link individual products to specific producers so that the consumer can connect with the grower or stitcher of the product they are holding in their hands. In short, the correct avenue for you depends on your consumer—where they are most likely to receive and retain information—as well as what resources you have at your disposal. A large multinational firm will most likely have a larger budget to spend on campaigns, whereas a start-up will need to be laser-focused on its efforts. With its ability to segment marketing, this is one reason why social media and Internet search advertising campaigns are so popular: they provide an increased likelihood to reach your target audience.

If your target audience is an investor, then you need a different course of action. This is where those investor-reporting methods discussed in Chapter 3 come into play. Asset managers are increasingly on the lookout for greenwashing, as they, too, are starting to be put under a microscope by regulators, particularly in Europe. As of February 2023, the Financial Conduct Authority, which regulates financial services firms in the United Kingdom, informed asset managers that between 2023 and 2024 it will launch an initiative to validate any ESG and sustainable-investing claims.[14] US firms are also under increased scrutiny, as exemplified by the SEC's decision to force BNY Mellon's Investment Adviser business to pay $1.5 million in penalties related to misstatements and omissions it had made regarding ESG considerations.[15] However, while consumers focus on specific products when deciding to make a purchase, investors tend to be more interested in the overall footprint or impact of a company as a whole. Brands have many different levers to pull in order to create positive metrics and need to consider all of them to present metrics their investors care about: worker wages, the environmental footprint of production, the use of sustainable raw materials, carbon footprint, partnerships with NGOs—the list goes on.

Decision #4: What

Because that list of levers to pull can feel endless, a brand needs to understand *what* it wants to highlight. Very few people want to fully understand how the sausage gets made; they are more interested in overall impact metrics, or how their individual purchase makes positive impact. This is why Allbirds (an impact native) publishes the carbon footprint of each pair of shoes right on the box for all to see. There is a clear, direct, and easily understood link between the brand's mission to create environmentally friendly footwear and the consumer seeing the impact they are having on the environment by buying that pair of shoes.

For impact immigrants, it can be tricky to message a new initiative or improvement, as you do not want your consumer or investor to assume you have not been creating positive impact all along. In our experience at Nest, we've seen many brands struggle to communicate how workers in their supply chains are finally making a living wage as a result of our partnership since the announcement causes consumers to wonder, "Wait, why weren't they earning that all along?" Obviously, consumers can't possibly appreciate just how much commitment goes into raising homeworkers' wages. They don't comprehend the full complexity of global supply chains, and there's no way to explain it in a single ad or on a very small hangtag. It is a positive impact story to be sure, and brands and producers should be able to get credit for their hard work and dedication. But these are tricky waters to navigate when it comes to discussions with the consumer. Think about what metrics are the most powerful to communicate to your consumer, combined with what makes the most sense for your brand story. With whom among your colleagues do you need to engage to make these decisions (aside from the communications and marketing teams, of course)?

In working with your internal teams and answering the important questions listed above, you should have a clear sense of what and how you would like to communicate. Now you need to make sure you choose messaging that does not greenwash.

The Nine Deadly Sins of Greenwashing

One challenge to identifying and avoiding greenwashing is that it can appear in many different ways. In 2011, buildinggreen.com, a company that acts as a "trusted source for guidance on healthy and sustainable products and strategies,"[16] published a list of the types of greenwashing that pervade the market,[17] and the list still resonates. Let's walk through their examples and explore how they can appear in practice so that you can keep an eye out, either as someone working for a brand or as a consumer.

Green by Association: This happens when a firm uses images and language to represent environmentally friendly approaches that have little or nothing to do with the company's operations. This is exactly what Chevron did with its problematic ads in the 1980s. A more recent example comes from the Swedish fast-fashion brand H&M. In 2019, they launched a marketing campaign filled with images of plants and vibrant greenery to advertise the launch of a new collection. The images of nature made one think of sustainability when in fact H&M's business model is extremely harmful to the environment. This type of greenwashing also occurs when a brand produces an item that *resembles* that of an environmentally focused product but shares none of its positive impact. In 2019 Amazon came out with a shoe that *looked* virtually identical to those Allbirds makes but lacked any of the sustainable production methods that makes Allbirds unique. The leadership of Allbirds received a lot of attention after publishing an editorial in which they urged Amazon to steal its sustainable production practices, not its design. The article even went so far as to offer sustainability tips for Amazon's future forays into footwear.[18]

Lack of Definition: This is when a brand proclaims positive benefits broadly that only apply to a very narrow set of criteria. For example, if the attributes of a product only present themselves in a controlled laboratory environment and could never be replicated in the real world. Technically, the product can do what is being claimed, just not for the person who is purchasing it.

Unproven Claims: This is where a brand makes claims without proof to back them up—no certifications from third parties and no evidence of the facts behind the claim. An example used by buildinggreen.com is when "a manufacturer claims to have eliminated hazardous ingredients from a product but claims that, due to trade secrets, it cannot reveal any specifics."[19] I often see this type of greenwashing take place when a brand is trying to keep up with its competitors who are making genuine strides in responsible sourcing. The pressure is too great to keep up with competition, so the greenwashing brand makes similar claims, perhaps in a lazy effort to try and save market share.

The Non Sequitur: This happens when a brand uses a proven fact about a product to claim that it does something else that is not relevant or does not make sense in context. For example, if a company advertises that a type of cleaner that kills bacteria can make everyone in the house live longer. Sure, it may kill bacteria on a countertop, potentially curbing the spread of colds and diseases. But to say that everyone will live longer as a result of buying that product? That is a bridge too far.

Forgetting the Life Cycle: This one is perhaps more complicated, as I believe it is often done unintentionally. In these examples, a brand proclaims that one of its products provides an environmental benefit without taking into consideration the energy and carbon needed to create the new product. A great example of this (unfortunately) is the movement to use cotton totes as shopping bags instead of plastic bags. Brands selling cotton reusable shopping bags often do not take into account the amount of resources that were required to produce those cotton bags: from the growing of the cotton to the spinning, weaving, and sewing, it turns out that it will take 7,100 uses of that bag before it becomes an environmentally friendly version of the conventional plastic bag.[20] Sorry to be the bearer of bad news on that one—I certainly have many of those reusable bags myself.

Bait and Switch: This happens when a brand successfully creates a product with positive impacts but then markets an entire family of products in the same way, even if they don't share those benefits. An example would be if a company marketed one environmentally friendly household cleaner but then designed similar labels and packaging for its other, non-eco-friendly, products and sold them alongside one another. In cases like this, it's better to celebrate the win on the one product rather than try to trick consumers into thinking the others are equally sustainable.

Rallying Behind a Lower Standard: We see this when a firm stands behind a certification but is also aware that the bar on that certification is pretty low. This often happens with certifications that are self-reported or lack the rigor and verification of third-party processes. Another example of this is programs that are "pay to play" certifications where products or companies are affiliated simply with membership fees. Unless a consumer is willing and able to do the research, how are they going to know that the seal on a product might actually be somewhat meaningless? One such model is the Sustainable Forestry Initiative, North America's largest forestry certification system. Most consumers are unaware that this program is actually backed by the logging industry and it has no rules for participants to meet any sort of sustainability criteria or on-site assessments to ensure that companies are being held to any sort of standard.[21]

Reluctant Enthusiast: This describes a company that publicly declares the importance of conservation and environmental sustainability but actively lobbies to try and ease government regulations related to their business practices. For example, when oil and gas companies make statements about the importance of conserving wildlife and forests while simultaneously pressuring the government to open more drilling sites in federally protected forests.

Outright Lying: This one is the most obvious and happens when a brand bends the truth to tell a false story. Think of a diamond company that claims it only uses conflict-free gems when, in reality, it is still sourcing "blood diamonds" from mines that are funding war crimes and slavery.

How Greenwashing Happens, and How to Avoid It

Motivations for greenwashing can come from three different categories:[22] external pressures, organizational structure, and internal biases. If things are out of balance and unaddressed in any of these, the likelihood of marketing missteps increases.

External pressures: Clearly the growing market demand for sustainable products and the pressure to keep up with competition are drivers for brand misbehavior in communications. Research conducted by the Economist Intelligence Unit (EIU)[23] discovered that on a global scale the search for sustainable goods rose 71% between 2016 and 2020. And, just as Unilever leveraged emerging economies as a driver for its success in the USLP, a lot of the growth in consumer interest reported by the EIU came from these same economies. If you are a brand being left behind, you may be more willing to stretch the truth regarding your sustainability to try and retain market share. Additionally, as mentioned in previous chapters, investors are increasingly looking at ESG rankings when making investment decisions, thus adding to that pressure. Finally, it has been relatively easy for brands to get away with greenwashing since, historically, there has been very little regulation or policing around it. Thankfully, this lack of accountability is starting to change with consumer and activist groups playing a much more vocal role in calling out companies in the court of public opinion. Greenpeace has been a thorn in the side of corporations since its founding in 1971, but now the Internet and social media give any individual the ability to become an activist as well. Meanwhile, governments are slowly beginning to shift—particularly in Europe— where regulators are starting to go after corporations and financial services companies for untruthful claims. Unfortunately, the penalties tend to be very small compared with the overall size of the businesses, and it is still rare for a company to get penalized by the government for misleading the public through its messaging.

Organizational structure: The way a firm is structured and the culture that it creates can also foster a breeding ground for poor marketing decisions. Incentive structures, communication pathways, and internal competition frameworks can all either encourage or prevent greenwashing. If a brand values profits over values and creates a bonus structure that rewards increased sales and market share above all else, then employees are more willing to do whatever it takes to get their numbers up. But if a firm leads with collaboration instead of internal competition, and ingrains corporate values of sustainability and impact into all new employees (think Patagonia), it is much less likely to encourage the stretching of the truth. In addition, if the marketing and communications team has easy access to information from those working on corporate responsibility and sustainable solutions or, better yet, uses that team to screen any public-facing communications and flag potentially misleading statements, the brand is less likely to present its efforts in an inauthentic way.

Individual biases: Human nature sometimes gets in the way here as well. We all tend to make statements related to goals, believing they are already a reality when the solution has yet to be developed. Combined with optimistic bias, or the tendency to envision positive outcomes much more frequently than negative ones, our human nature can be a recipe for misleading the public as to the true current state of an effort. One way to counteract these tendencies is to ensure that no one is making communication decisions in isolation. This can be difficult if the communication is coming directly from the CEO, but if enough structure is baked into the development of talking points and messaging, guardrails can be put in place across the firm.

The Next Frontier: Woke Washing

Similar to greenwashing, woke washing is the practice of using a social movement to increase product sales without addressing how a brand is either complicit in the issue or actively engaged in creating a solution. During the rise of protests and important national dialogue spurred by the Black Lives Matter movement in 2020, many companies were blacking out their social media channels to show support. However, these types of communications, without any action behind them, fell flat and were deemed performative. Even worse, brands were using the movement to try and sell product. The most famous example of this type of "woke washing" was Pepsi's infamous commercial that depicted Kendall Jenner leading a large group of people to confront a row of battle-ready police offers. After Jenner handed one of the officers an icy-cold can of Pepsi, all tension between protesters and law enforcement disappeared.[24] This was Pepsi's "Chevron ad" moment, and consumers vehemently criticized the brand for their feeble attempt at solidarity. Instead, consumers responded favorably to the brands that were actively engaged in dialogue with the community, committing to the 15% pledge of leveraging shelf space for BIPOC businesses, raising funds to support BLM efforts, and verbalizing other ways in which they were working to fight systemic racism such as creating more equity on their boards or establishing leadership development programs for their BIPOC employees.

Aligning Values with Action

It is not enough for companies to want to align themselves with a movement—whether it involves social justice, environmental impact, or responsible sourcing. They must first decide what they stand for and how they want to enact change. These commitments must be matched with quantifiable and measurable metrics that help achieve, and then eventually communicate, progress on those goals. "Companies need to thoughtfully explore the lanes in which they are truly willing to make a commitment to creating change for the better, with clear outcomes in mind," says James Walker, whom I quoted at the start of this chapter. There needs to be true alignment across the company and associated stakeholders, and your communications team can be one of your chief advocates and thought partners in that journey. Why? As Walker states, "Because we're concerned with the actions businesses take, the story those actions will tell, and the positive or negative impact that results from the meaning our key stakeholders take away. Do we win all the time? No. But more CEOs are seeing the value, and more are listening."

Now that you understand all the factors and risks at play with communicating your sustainability and impact initiatives, hopefully you can move forward in developing a strategy that avoids the many pitfalls so many brands encounter.

9

Convincing the Money Folks: Business Finance for Sustainability and Impact

"The budget is not just a collection of numbers, but an expression of our values and aspirations."
                        —Jack Lew, former US Secretary of the Treasury

AT SOME POINT along your responsible-sourcing journey, you may come across colleagues or managers who, while they appreciate the point of sustainability efforts, still do not believe that responsible sourcing is a sound financial decision. In order to remove the road-block and gain access to the working capital you need to help meet your objectives, you will need to convince your finance team, or other internal colleagues or departments, that impact initiatives are good for business. Speaking as a chief financial officer, I can admit that the finance team is often the most skeptical when it comes to allocating funds for new projects, particularly those, such as sustainability, where initial investments might be significant and the impact on consumer, the environment, or the supply chain might take longer to realize.

Throughout the course of this book, we have looked at how consumer behavior is driving increased participation in impact and sustainability within business. Based on this trend, if you engage in responsible-sourcing activities, you will be rewarded with increased customer loyalty, increased market share (in the form of new customers you converted from your competitors), and/or customers willing to pay more for your products. In other words, responsible sourcing should increase your overall revenues. However, the finance team may still look askance at you when you try to convince them of this because they know that increased responsibility will invariably increase your firm's expenses in the short term, even if they are offset by increased revenues in the longer term. For example, if your organization launches an initiative to help raise wages for factory workers, won't you end up spending more to source these now more expensive products? Or if you commit to becoming carbon neutral, won't you need to spend money to invest in the technologies required to reduce your carbon footprint? How will your firm absorb those costs? Will you still be able to earn a profit, or will you just break even after all the hard work?

The good news is that there are several avenues you can use to help prove the financial argument for responsible sourcing, looking at how your firm is able to access capital. In addition, the focus on ESG (environmental, social, and governance) and United Nations Sustainable Development Goal (UNSDG) metrics are driving a significant amount of innovation when it comes to how funds can be accessed and allocated within supply chains. Before detailing these innovations, we should start with a brief primer on supply chain finance more generally.

The Basics of Supply Chain Finance

When a brand places an order from a producer, they rarely pay any money for the items up front. Instead, they provide net payment terms in which they pay the producer only after the brand takes possession of the product. Even then, payment is not instantaneous. Normally the brand pays 60, 90, even 120 days after they receive the goods, and their policy can have significant financial impacts on the producer's business. Let's say I own a factory in India that makes dining chairs. I receive an order from an American big-box retailer for 25,000 units. Once I receive the purchase-order paperwork, I am required to deliver the chairs. Best-case scenario, those chairs have already been produced and are sitting in one of my warehouses waiting to get sold. This means they can get loaded into a container and shipped to the United States. Worst-case scenario, without any upfront payment, I need to purchase the raw materials and invest in the labor costs to produce and ship those 25,000 units. Sometimes, the brand takes ownership of the chairs right at the docks; other times, they do so only once the chairs reach the brand distribution center. In this case, the chairs must get loaded off the boat and onto a truck (or train) and travel to the distribution center before the clock on the net-payment term starts. Either way, I, as the producer, am going to have to wait two to four months before I can expect the buyer to process my payment. This presents a problem because I have already spent all my capital to make the product, capital (aka working capital) that I could be using to manufacture new orders, pay my workers, and generally run my business. This lag time means production facilities must be large enough to manage the cash flow required by these generally unfavorable terms.

Thankfully, a solution to this problem has been around for centuries (truly—there is evidence of trade finance dating back to Babylonian clay tablets from 3000 BCE).[1] The most common current iteration is called supply chain finance (also known as factoring, or reverse factoring, depending on the structure and whether a loan insurer is involved). Here is essentially how it works: once I send my invoice for the chairs to the brand, I am able to get money immediately from a financial institution that is partnered with the brand. I get a slightly reduced amount of money (since the bank takes a percentage) in exchange for this convenience. Then, after the 60–120 days elapses and it comes time for the brand to process payment, they pay the bank the full amount of the invoice instead of paying me.

You are probably wondering why I, as the owner of the chair business, would do this. If I wanted money, why not take a business loan from my local bank instead of going through the brand's financial partner? The reason is because I am able to get a much better interest rate with the brand's bank because they are using the brand's credit rating, not mine, to calculate it. And, if my transaction is with a very large firm—such as the big-box retailer in my case—they will most likely have a far better credit rating than my smaller international production facility. When looking at the risk of a transaction, the lender is generally more interested in the risk of the brand not paying them versus me not delivering the chairs. So, even though I get less than the full invoice, I now have the working capital I need to run my business and move on to the next order without the time-intensive need to seek traditional bank loans on my own. In short, supply-chain financing lowers the interest rate I get charged when taking out a loan while giving me the money I need, when I need it, to help grow my business.

Innovations in Supply Chain Finance

If this type of solution has been around for centuries, how is it now encouraging increased impact and responsible sourcing? This is where things have been getting interesting, and there are two types of initiatives that I want to highlight: CSR-driven supply-chain financing and the financing of small-scale producers.

In Chapter 3, I referenced how Puma developed an Environmental Profit & Loss Statement, which measured their environmental impact across all aspects of its business. In looking at that data, the team at Puma realized something important: a significant portion of their environmental impact was occurring outside of its core operations facilities (e.g. its corporate offices, warehouses, and stores). In fact, a whopping 94% of it came from parts of the supply chain that the business did not actively control, namely from its production partners and the acquisition of raw materials.[2] If Puma (or any other brand, for that matter) wants to significantly meet its sustainability objectives, it needs help from these partners. In their quest to be leading edge in sustainability efforts, Puma had already developed corporate sustainability and responsibility metrics and scorecards for its producers to help them make sourcing decisions and engage in supply chain transparency. And, like most brands (responsible ones and not), Puma was already engaged in traditional forms of supply chain finance. What if it combined these elements to encourage further action at the producer level?

In 2016, alongside financing partner BNP Paribas, Puma launched a supply-chain financing option that rewarded producers who performed well on its responsibility scorecards with below-standard interest rates on any financing they received from the company. This meant that if a producer made investments into their factories to reduce emissions or create more environmentally friendly production practices, it would receive a discount on any capital it needed to access. Meanwhile, producers that were falling behind in their sustainability objectives would be charged slightly higher-than-standard interest rates. Why would the laggards be willing to accept these higher rates instead of trying to seek financing elsewhere? Because, through Puma, they could leverage the corporation's high credit rating, which meant the production facility still received a better deal than it could get on its own. The beauty of this innovation is its design: it uses a form of finance that is readily understood and has been in practice for centuries (supply chain finance), but it rewards top performers and encourages them to continue investing in their sustainability efforts while pressuring the laggards to keep up. The historic alternative used to be that a brand, such as Puma, would need to resort to extremes, such as eliminating their contracts and moving production elsewhere, when production partners did not comply to their auditing requirements. Puma wins by moving the needle on its sustainability objectives in a way that is responsible to its sourcing partners, and sourcing partners get rewarded for innovating and investing in sustainability. BNP Paribas is still able to make a market return on these loans, since the higher rates charged to the poor performers offset the lower rates charged to the top ones. BNP Paribas does not need to ask any of its investors (who are generally looking for a market return) for forgiveness or convince them to embark on an initiative that may seem philanthropic in nature. While brands such as Puma and financial institutions such as BNP Paribas piloted this idea,* it has now grown into a model that is rewarding vendors who make social impact and environmental improvements. It is an innovative and rewarding way to encourage change by leveraging market forces instead of solely relying on philanthropy. Oftentimes, the capital required to make improvements is a major roadblock to improving production systems. This model helps address that hurdle for brands and producers alike.

The second initiative I want to highlight addresses the limitations of traditional supply-chain financing models. The established framework of supply chain finance as outlined above (factoring and/or reverse factoring) is great, but it is designed to work well for larger-scale manufacturing and for production processes that do not take a lot of time. What about supply chains that rely on smaller-scale producers (such as coffee farmers) or small and medium-sized enterprises (such as the craft sector), where producers may be operating within the informal economy, have limited credit history, or lack understanding of financial services? Traditional finance institutions have been extremely hesitant to work within these sectors, leaving a void to be filled by a new type of lending. Enter Root Capital. Founded in 1999 by Willy Foote, Root Capital is a nonprofit organization that focuses on agricultural businesses in rural areas of Latin America, Southeast Asia, and sub-Saharan Africa. It works with farming cooperatives to provide working capital through affordable financing. The organization is structured as a nonprofit because it serves as much more than a bank. In 2021, in addition to lending $148.3 million to farming communities, they dedicated more than 4,000 days' worth of time to train farmers in their geographies of

---

* There were a few other brands with similar projects, such as Levi Strauss.

interest on critical business skills and strategy.[3] This additional support helped farmers improve their yields and, thus, their overall business performance. Another reason Root Capital operates as a nonprofit is so it can use a blended capital model (combining philanthropy with traditional investment dollars) to take riskier bets and spend more time performing due diligence to ensure a cooperative is ready to engage in a lending partnership. Just as at Nest, where we often work with businesses that have not been trained in compliance before, the Root Capital team enters communities that may have never been educated on business acumen or the ins and outs of business lending. This type of work takes time—a cost that would not be covered under traditional lending. In addition, Root Capital can use philanthropy to deploy something called first-loss capital. Since they are taking riskier business bets (according to Root's own reporting, 83% of their 2020 loans filled credit needs unmet by traditional lenders)[4] there is a higher chance that loan recipients may not be able to fully repay their loans within the expected time frame. If this happens, philanthropy steps in and offsets that cost of lost capital, so that Root Capital can continue lending to new communities. Based on their impact numbers, the model has been very successful. Since its founding Root Capital has lent $1.6 billion to under-served enterprises, and their clients have had an annual revenue growth of 25%.[5]

Even with these innovations, there are still populations being left behind. As you think about your responsible-sourcing footprint, consider that, in some cases, it might make sense to use philanthropy instead of traditional financing to fund a business opportunity. For example, at Nest we are currently piloting a model to provide working capital through recoverable grants supported by the Tory Burch Foundation. We have found that, in certain communities in the United States, there is often an aversion toward traditional lending. This is particularly true among BIPOC makers as well as women makers. The makers we work with—mainly independent owner-operators, also known as "solopreneurs"—are wary of taking on any sort of credit risk when it comes to securing working capital for their business. In the United States, small-scale business owners like these often take on *personal* credit risk as opposed to being shielded behind a corporation. Because of this, we at Nest have had to rethink how we provide working capital. Instead of a loan, we distribute the funding as grants where a failure to pay back will not damage the recipient's credit score. Still, we encourage the maker businesses to repay if and when they meet their business objectives through a pay-it-forward type of approach. This way, the business gets the experience of accounting for the working capital and begins to build the habit of repayment. This model is particularly impactful as participants can help provide a pool of funding that gets recycled to other makers by paying back their loans following business success. Like Root Capital, we also provide resources such as business-acumen training, monthly consulting and check-ins, and networking opportunities to establish deeper connections to other makers. As of this writing, Nest's working-capital program is still in the pilot phase, but we have already found that the makers who participate appreciate the capital but are often even more thankful for the financial education and connections.

Other Finance Innovations

The advancement of technology and digital currency provides yet another opportunity for innovations in lending. New platforms (both blockchain and non-blockchain) are enabling greater transaction transparency and are aiding lenders in supporting small and midsize enterprises (SMEs), particularly those in emerging markets and those that are currently unbanked. To that end, since 2018

Accion, a nonprofit organization committed to giving people the financial tools they need to improve their lives, has partnered with the Mastercard Center for Inclusive Growth to build a stronger network of digital financing providers geared toward micro, small, and medium-sized enterprises across 22 countries. Their effort has leveraged the work of 47 financial technology companies and nine financial service providers and has impacted 4.4 million small businesses.[6]

Whether you are sourcing from mass manufacturers, farmers, or global SMEs, supply-chain financing is one lever you can pull to positively increase your impact, while simultaneously benefiting your suppliers. There are myriad options for you to consider that would allow your producers to access lower-cost financing options to help them pay for any upgrades necessary to increase your impact. The approach you choose depends on your brand strategy, what types of populations you source from, and how creative you can get in leveraging traditional solutions.

Another option is to seek to lower your own cost of capital through new offerings in corporate debt. Just as BNP Paribas offered Puma producers lower interest rates if they performed well under Puma's sustainability metrics, brands themselves can take advantage of increased opportunities to receive a lower interest rate on business loans if they meet predetermined sustainability and impact goals. The first time I became aware of this was in 2019, when the luxury fashion brand Prada announced an agreement with Crédit Agricole to secure a five-year sustainability-based term loan valued at 50 million euros, the first of its kind within the luxury industry.[7] If during that five-year period, Prada achieved LEED Gold or Platinum certification in a certain number of stores, provided a set number of training hours for employees on sustainable practices, and met targets for using a sustainable nylon substitute called

Re-Nylon in the production of its apparel, Crédit Agricole would reduce its interest rates, thereby lowering its cost of capital.

This type of arrangement has since been replicated many times, and the COVID-19 pandemic also accelerated the use of impact bonds to address social issues. One of the largest examples came from goliath Alphabet (parent company of Google), which in August 2020 announced it was offering $5.75 billion in bonds to investors as a way to help finance the company's sustainability and impact projects. The goals set forth by the company included environmental ones, such as continued moves toward clean energy and transportation, as well as commitments to social and economic issues such as affordable housing, racial equity, and support for small businesses negatively impacted by COVID-19.[8]

What excites me most about impact-based bonds is that they are a great way to help pay for capital projects while, ideally, helping companies save money in the future. A company can use proceeds from the sale of these bonds to acquire physical assets, such as solar panels or fleets of electric vehicles, or make other supply chain improvements that require a substantial expenditure up front. But these investments will also help pay for themselves over time through reduced energy costs and other efficiencies.

Convincing Skeptics through Metrics

What if your finance team remains unconvinced? You need an analytical approach, one that the numbers-driven folks will be able to process. You can find this in the Return on Sustainable Investment (ROSI) tool developed by Tensie Whelan and the team at the Center for Sustainable Business at the New York University Stern School of Business.[9] Tools such as ROSI can be extremely helpful in translating supply chain sustainability and impact goals into language that the CFO will understand. It follows a five-step process, the first of which involves identifying what your firm currently does related to sustainability or what you are aiming to do. Through interviews and data gathering across the organization, you can establish documentation that outlines all sustainability issues in order of importance according to your stakeholders. This can be a firm-wide effort, or it could focus solely on supply chain and sourcing practices.

The second step is to examine what operational or management practices have changed over time in order to address sustainability targets, or what practices you are seeking to change with a new initiative. Oftentimes, these have not been formally documented, so listing them out is a key step. Think back to the Unilever example. The firm was able to achieve success by carefully monitoring what was working within the brands leading the USLP so that the information could then be distributed across the corporation.

The next two steps are to think through nonmonetary benefits that are a part of your goal and how to quantify those benefits. Reduction in greenhouse gas emissions? Establishment of a circular economy for your product? You need to know what you are aiming to change so as to narrow the focus of the work and to work toward the financial implications as well. Once you have that list of goals, you will need to price it out by using some sort of established benchmark in order to determine the monetary value of your effort. To illustrate, let's look at an example that the NYU team provided. When measuring the value of sustainable ranching practices, they looked at the reduced number of acres needed, the change in cost of renting the land, the amount of beef sold before and after the shift to sustainable farming, and the difference in price between conventional and sustainable beef.

The final step in the process is to calculate all the cost savings to determine the monetary value of the effort. This can then get plugged into a calculation often used in corporate finance—present value of future cash flows—which I will discuss below. The ROSI methodology has been implemented across sectors ranging from automotive manufacturing to agriculture to fashion. Working with the luxury brand Eileen Fisher,[10] the NYU team was able to demonstrate that by shifting product shipment methods from air freight to sea and trucking, the brand spent $1.6 million less in transportation costs while simultaneously reducing its carbon footprint. And, by incorporating a new in-store garment recycling program (not dissimilar to the Patagonia approach), Eileen Fisher created a net benefit of $1.8 million while diverting clothing from landfills. Both are strong win-wins, to be sure, and numbers that most certainly can be utilized in corporate-finance calculations to further make your case with the CFO.

If you have studied corporate finance, a requirement for most MBA programs, you may be familiar with the idea of the present value of future cash flows, which helps teams assess whether to invest in a new initiative. Looking at in the simplest terms possible, the concept can be thought of in two ways. First, what do you need to *earn* in revenue in the future, and how long will it take to break even on the financial investment you make today? Second, what do you need to *save* in reduced costs in the future, and how long will it take to break even? In both cases, what is an acceptable rate of return (or cost savings) from your project? One of the factors in the calculation here is the weighted average cost of capital (WACC)—the higher the WACC, the higher your rate of return needs to be. Therefore, by meeting your sustainability objectives and lowering the interest rate on your corporate debt through a sustainability-linked loan, you have succeeded on lowering your WACC and consequently need a lower rate of return to provide a viable business opportunity for your finance team to consider. This is somewhat of an oversimplification (there are plenty of textbooks on corporate finance if you want to dive deeper), but it is important to note that businesses tend to have a predetermined acceptable rate of return (referred to as the "hurdle rate") required before they approve a project. What is interesting about these sustainability and impact initiatives is that, because they are also helping meet UNSDGs or ESG objectives and are deemed beneficial to investors, brands are lowering their hurdle rate when it comes to approving these types of projects; the decision is increasingly not just about dollars and cents, or how long it takes to break even. As long as you can demonstrate with quantifiable metrics that your investment in sustainability and impact makes financial sense over the long term, you should have an easier time getting approvals from your CFO.

Putting the Pieces of the Puzzle Together

Corporate finance is just one more piece in the puzzle, combined with supply chain transparency, innovation, strategic partnerships, and communications. Success really boils down to how you use all of these elements together, based on your personal and corporate context. At this point, you hopefully have the knowledge you need to embark—or continue—on your responsible-sourcing journey. Our final chapter will talk through the steps you need to take, and factors to consider, as you become a changemaker in your own organization.

10

On Your Own Path

"Every great dream begins with a dreamer. Always remember, you have within you the strength, the patience, and the passion to reach for the stars to change the world."

—Harriet Tubman

I WROTE THIS book as an introduction to responsible sourcing for both consumers and corporate changemakers. Together we have examined how events in recent history have shaped both thinking and behavior around responsible sourcing for corporations and consumers. These events have also spurred forward the tools, technologies, and strategies that companies can leverage in order to increase transparency, accountability, and sustainability in their supply chains. We have also highlighted how this continues to be a rapidly changing area of business. New innovations; new partnerships; new motivations and attitudes by consumers, investors, and regulators; and even new risks (such as COVID-19) continue to shape our attitudes in ways both anticipated and surprising.

The logical question to ask as we conclude our discussion is: what now? How can you stay abreast of the shifting landscape of responsible sourcing, and how can you start working to create change inside your own department, brand, and organization? In this final chapter, I will walk through where I think the sector is heading in the foreseeable future, as well as some suggestions of how you can navigate change within your own career. Given that responsible sourcing is not just a sustainability and impact problem but a power and politics one as well, this latter consideration is critical. I will also share some of the resources that I use on a regular basis to stay informed on trends and opportunities.

Where We Are Going

With our environment ever-changing, it is anyone's guess as to what responsible business will look like a few decades from now. While futurists abound with hypotheses and best guesses, I will share some of my personal predictions here.

I believe many future advancements will manifest in three broad categories: environmental (fueled by increased attention to and impacts being felt by climate change), social justice (fueled by increased awareness of the disparities inherent in our world, plus the rise of accountability culture in which missteps by corporations can be shared widely and rapidly), and technology. The organizations that take all these things into consideration when deciding their strategies will have a huge competitive advantage while also setting new standards of practice to lead change in the future.

Environmental Concerns

Investments of time, capital, and brain power will continue to be poured into tech-based solutions for reducing negative environmental impacts, leading to both new innovations and new broader-scale partnerships. Companies such as EVRNU, which we discussed in Chapter 6, that provide sourcing alternatives for the reuse of existing materials, will find ways to scale their capabilities and create an accessible and viable price point for their services. This will push their work beyond the smaller-scale pilot programs we are seeing with brands such as Zara and create an opportunity for full collections of fabrics to rely on the technology. We will continue to see a rise in circular-economy design efforts, and brands such as Adidas and Allbirds will share even more of their innovations with others, making it easier for more companies to start on their own innovative design efforts.

Thanks to favorable financing opportunities, firms will be able to reduce their carbon footprints through capital projects, such as replacing their delivery fleets with electric vehicles or upgrading their offices and warehouses with solar panels. Both governments and sourcing partners who want to improve their environmental P&Ls will pressure polluting factories to clean up their acts.

Social Justice and the Pursuit of Equity

As societies grapple with both the imbalances of power inherent in globalization and the need for equity and inclusion here at home, companies will turn to responsible sourcing as a way to demonstrate their values and participation in the global conversation around equity. Brands will increasingly be required (through both regulation and consumer expectation) to drill down to the last mile of their supply chains—those previously invisible actors like Laurie in the Philippines—to ensure every worker is treated and paid fairly. Standards and auditing systems will enable further transparency, and organizations such as Nest, which help firms understand their full supply chains, will become even busier. Technology solutions will scale these efforts as well—leveraging new platforms to bring greater visibility and voice to global workforces and long, complex supply chains from raw materials to shelf.

From a financial transparency perspective, the work of BanQu and efforts from the Mastercard Center for Inclusive Growth will continue to pay dividends (pun intended) to the world's unbanked. Increased visibility into the payment received and conditions experienced by last-mile producers—whether it's a farmer, a waste picker, or a small-scale artisan—will continue to increase brand responsibility regarding the welfare of workers around the world. Greater visibility also means increased consumer knowledge about workers driving forward pressure on firms to sustain these human-centered efforts.

At home, increased transparency into and conversations around wages and the experiences of marginalized groups within our society will continue to drive action at the corporate level regarding racial equity and opportunity. Black Lives Matter, as well as other movements focused on exposing and eradicating prejudices against minority groups, will continue to gain traction and push for accountability. The more awareness these movements receive and the more educated the public becomes, the more pressure brands will feel to behave ethically and equitably across all areas of their business: from whom they appoint to leadership positions to whom they source product from. I believe that consumers will increasingly support businesses who demonstrate their commitments to racial and social equity and use their dollars to support antiracist, or denounce racist, behavior. Hashtags and sleek ad campaigns are no longer enough; companies will need to reinforce their commitments to social justice with real, verifiable actions.

Future Disasters

Of course, it would be naïve to believe that, just because society is trending toward sustainability and equity, we won't make mistakes along the way. Additional wake-up calls are somewhat inevitable (not even I will hazard a guess as to what the next Rana Plaza or COVID-19 may be). I believe that corporations will continue to react as quickly as possible, utilizing coalitions and cross-sector efforts to address these new challenges and work to ensure that both business and society can limit future risk. With the ever-increasing information flow provided by social media, consumer eyes will be readily fixed on the corporations that make missteps in both their behavior and in their messaging.

The Benefits and Perils of Technology

Even as I'm finishing up this book, I see new technologies emerging that have the potential to radically shift how we produce and source products. Advancements in artificial intelligence and the increased presence of robotics in manufacturing will change the dynamics of globalization. As we discussed early in the book, globalization and outsourcing of production was often spurred by the chase for cheaper labor. Technological innovations are enabling the acquisition of robots at lower costs just at a time when bringing manufacturing back to developed economies in order to lower carbon footprint is increasing in its appeal. These combined make the nearshoring of manufacturing not just appealing but likely. Even when the production stays abroad, increased automation is all but assured to change the face of the workforce. If a factory no longer needs to employ thousands of workers, who have been replaced by machines and a core staff in the hundreds to run and maintain them, what type of employment will become available for workers that do not have advanced degrees in business or robotics? And what happens to the workforce in emerging economies if those factories eventually shut down? I believe that this is an area of responsibility that will be felt by corporations and governments in the near future. Solutions— such as a universal basic income in which every citizen of working age would receive a monthly check, regardless of their employment status—are already being discussed. The issue still feels somewhat dystopian or like science fiction at the moment, but unless new employment opportunities get created as a result of other new sectors such as green energy solutions, we will face a shortage of viable jobs for a large percentage of the global population.

Artificial intelligence will also play a role in the reduction of overall goods being manufactured, as it will lead to a more customized, made-to-order approach particularly in the garment industry.

Already there are companies that have body scanning technology to measure for precise fit. With the punch of a few keyboard strokes, this body scan information could travel right to the factory floor, where those robots mentioned above stand at the ready to produce the precise garment you want. As consumer tastes trend away from overconsumption, hyper-customization could be the next frontier to capture market share while simultaneously producing fewer wasted garments and therefore fewer items that end in the landfill.

Artisanal Work and Repair

By contrast to the labor challenges of technology outlined above, I feel that the handcraft sector may actually thrive because of robotics—the human touch in craft production is something that is valued by the consumer and oftentimes is impossible for a machine to replicate (at least right now). I can see the continued rise in handcraft production and purchasing as one way to bring economic opportunities to rural and underserved communities. Additionally, the rise in conversations around circularity in production means a steady increase in the number of companies looking to build repair-based programs and/or find purposeful ways to use waste material. These liability programs will thrive on artisanal labor and be difficult to automate in the short term.

From the Corporation to the Individual: Power, Politics, and How to Make Change

I want to acknowledge that, as an individual, the considerations in this book might feel overwhelming. How can you, as a member of an organization, accelerate change in a positive direction? And just as importantly, how can you pursue responsible sourcing without sacrificing your own career? Through my work, I have had the privilege of witnessing committed people navigate their careers well and have observed some common themes.

Before you take your first step, consider your place and power within the organization. A CSO or CFO has a lot more power (and experience) than, say, a marketing manager. But the latter can still make an impact within their own job description. For example, perhaps as a marketing manager, you can educate yourself on greenwashing and serve as a quality control on marketing messages that might read as pandering or untruthful. Or you might think of how to play up a sustainability angle in a new product launch and then measure how that message is received. A lower-level accountant can research how switching to a more energy efficient production method will save the company money and then run it up the chain of command (recall our discussion on the present value of future cash flows in Chapter 9). If nothing else, this book has shown how sustainability is a competitive advantage, so anyone who can help the company perform better through creative sustainability solutions will not only help the company but ultimately succeed in their own career.

Getting Started

Once you determine that you wish to create more responsible practices in your organization, start by looking for the low-hanging fruit rather than trying to uproot and replant the whole tree. This serves two functions: it can help you get a quick win and demonstrate to skeptics that your efforts are not a waste of time. And it can help you learn how to navigate the political structure and culture of your organization without having to also solve a complicated problem, giving you invaluable lessons as you look to build on successes. Ensure that this first foray into sustainability and impact clearly aligns with the priorities of your brand and the focus of your customer: for initial pilots the direct link between business and profit and responsibility should be obvious. If you need some help encouraging action in your company, look at what your direct competitors are doing. Is there something they are doing that, if successful, will result in your losing market share? Nothing motivates naysayers like a threat to the bottom line. A few other tips to keep in mind:

- Focus on your company's competencies. Now is not the time to create new product lines, but instead leverage your core products. Remember that product longevity—figuring out how a product can last longer or be recycled more successfully—*is* a sustainability strategy. How can you improve an existing product? Can you create a recycling or buy-back program? Reduce the amount or change the type of packaging used?

- You can only manage what you can measure. As you look at those core competencies, leverage tools, such as ROSI, that can help you with your analysis. Get personally versed in sustainability, impact, and ESG reporting. Look at what firms are doing regarding environmental and impact P&Ls. You may not be able to institute an effort to create your own impact P&L in your current role, but you at least will be speaking the language understood by your finance teams and start connecting the dots for the decision makers. Find your passion, and do the deep dives into research and content.

- Find your tribe of like-minded people both internally and externally. Collaborate with colleagues to help give more voice and power to your goals. And, while you are doing it all, remember that you still need to please the boss. Not much change can take place if you ruffle too many feathers and find yourself out of a job.

When You Are the Boss

If you are fortunate enough to get that corner office, your role in the sustainability journey shifts a bit. You are now positioned to empower and energize others to help implement responsible sourcing, and you can pull different levers than the ones you had access to while you were working your way up through the ranks.

Firstly, you can send a clear message to your team by revisiting incentive structures. Reward the hard work by providing bonuses based on overall company performance in meeting sustainability and impact objectives, as opposed to just rewarding based on individual performance metrics. Build in gamification and a culture of healthy competition so as to encourage innovation and commitment to making the hard changes. Think through ways the company can band together and celebrate milestone achievements, such as pursuing and achieving B Corp certification, or adopting new standards such as the Nest Seal of Ethical Handcraft. It is important to keep the team inspired, particularly when they are working on complicated, long-term approaches to solving systemic challenges.

Secondly, work to redefine your firm's view on the ROI (return on investment) of projects. Establish your own environmental and impact P&Ls, determine the cost of carbon to your business, and change the hurdle rates required for capital projects when there is a sustainability or impact lens on the proposed program. Utilize patient capital to ease some of the pressure to deliver profits right away, taking the Polman approach. Leverage sustainability and impact bonds to lower your cost of capital through all this work.

Above all, as a leader of your firm, focus on your business strategy and the culture that you set. When thinking about purpose before profit, you still need to think about growth. As you embrace sustain-ability and impact, what choices will you have to make in order to commit to responsible sourcing? Will you need to pivot out of prod-uct lines that are particularly or inherently fraught with concerns or negative impacts? If so, what product lines will your firm want to lean more heavily into to make up for that loss in revenue? Where will growth come from in the future? You will need to stay abreast of consumer trends, technological innovations, and new design and production capabilities to plan your points of differentiation.

While you tackle the business strategy, it will also be important for you to not make a common misstep when it comes to company culture: embracing hero culture instead of collaborative leadership and collective action. At first glance one might think that hero culture is the best way to quickly achieve success, as it is defined as an "organization that is run by a group of hard-working, highly talented 'heroes' on sheer strength, will and knowledge."[1] As the leader of the organization, you will have the expertise, the network and connections, and the decision-making power to force through change, bending the company to your vision. Becoming the hero, if you will. But how effective is that? Think back to Polman and Chouinard. Did either of them move mountains all by themselves or insulated leadership circles? Absolutely not. On the contrary, they both, in their own ways, developed plans for collective action and collaborative leadership. In these models they created a cul-ture of sharing information and equally shouldering burdens. And while Polman and Chouinard were typically the ones making pub-lic declarations about their companies' goals, everyone who worked for them understood that they too had an important role in which they could contribute to those common objectives. Together, all were able to celebrate in the accomplishments. This type of culture breeds more rapid information by pooling expertise, more lasting change by distributing the knowledge and ownership more equally, and more loyalty to the mission.* Lorna Davis, a former leader at Kraft and Modelez and former CEO of Danone North America, has a powerful Ted Talk on this topic.[2]

Some Helpful Resources

No matter where you are on your journey, you are going to need additional information in this very dynamic space. There are undoubtedly countless places to turn, but here are some of my more frequent reference points. These, like the landscape, are changing all the time—be vigilant on new avenues of information and inspiration.

Blogs and E-newsletters   Depending on your area of passion, seek out and subscribe to the blogs and newsletters that you find most relevant. One of my favorite resources is *reconsidered.co*, curated by Jessica Marati Radparvar, a social impact and sustainability consultant who has experience working within leading edge firms such as PVH and Eileen Fisher. The newsletter is a great monthly compilation of stories around sustainability and impact, and the team curates a reading list of top books on the subject as well (not to mention a jobs board if you are looking to make a pivot). Company-specific and research-focused newsletters are also often a wealth of information, particularly those that are leading edge in their approach or research. Some of my frequent reads are: The Mastercard Center for Inclusive Growth, McKinsey (you can filter for content specifically related to sustainability and ESG topics), Reuters (again filtering for ESG content), Elevate (an auditing firm), as well as from organizations such as BSR (Businesses for Social Responsibility), New York University's Center for Sustainable Business, and the Stanford Social Innovation Review.

---

* For more information on this subject, check out the powerful TED Talk by Lorna Davis, former executive at Kraft and Mondelez and former CEO of Danone North America, https://www.ted.com/talks/lorna_davis_a_guide_to_collaborative_leadership.

LinkedIn   LinkedIn is particularly useful, as you can follow both thought leaders in the space as well as competitors and companies you admire. Inevitably, by following one you will be exposed to entirely new leaders and new conversations. It is an easy way to follow countless numbers of chief sustainability officers, industry visionaries such as Paul Polman, as well as brands that are doing responsible sourcing right. The platform's hashtag functionality is another great way to get exposed to new avenues of communication around the subject.

Take a Class   Lean into being a lifetime learner (believe me, I have made a career out of it) and educate yourself on responsible sourcing as well as the key business concepts that will help bolster your ability to create change. If you do not have a finance background, consider an introduction to corporate finance course so you can better understand the concerns and metrics CFOs use to determine the best ways to invest a firm's money. Or you might study macroeconomics to gain understanding of the trends in globalization. If you work in accounting, you might take a course on branding or marketing to improve your communication around the issues that are important to you. If a full MBA program is not possible (I certainly understand the time and capital commitment required there), you can still find the resources you need through continuing education platforms, found in online business school executive education and certificate programs. It is a lot easier to weed out the noise and greenwashing if you understand fundamental business concepts.

Going Old School: Hitting the Books   The list of books that have influenced my journey is growing by the day, and the titles I provide here are by no means exhaustive. Rather, they are a good start for you to consider as you think about next steps.

Cradle to Cradle: Remaking the Way We Make Things, by Michael Braungart and William McDonough. A book about rethinking the design process to create more of a circular economy.

Poor Economics: A Radical Rethinking of the Way to Fight Global Poverty, by Abhijit Banerjee and Esther Duflo. An eye-opener for me in terms of how both philanthropy and business can drive greater impact with the global impoverished.

Conscious Capitalism: Liberating the Heroic Spirit of Business, by John Mackey (co-CEO of Whole Foods) and Raj Sisodia. A helpful way of showing how a business can drive both growth and impact.

Net Positive: How Courageous Companies Thrive by Giving More than They Take, by Paul Polman and Andrew Winston. A peek inside the mind of Polman, and a deep dive into his philosophy and approach related to sustainability in business.

Chief Sustainability Officers at Work: How CSOs Build Successful Sustainability and ESG Strategies, by Chrissa Pagitsas. A series of more than 20 interviews with the CSOs of top 500 companies, discussing how they set and execute some of the strategies we have discussed in this book.

Green Swans: The Coming Boom in Regenerative Capitalism, by John Elkington. A discussion of how investment will play a role in developing the much-needed increase in sustainability and impact to save people and planet.

Now, It Is Up to You

Writing this book has been quite possibly the most challenging thing I have ever done. How do you put down on paper years of life experience and research? But it has also been one of the most thrilling, thanks to you. I hope you walk away from this book with both a better understanding of what responsible sourcing means but also having started formulating your own plan of action. The more informed you are, the more informed your decisions can be, and the more power you have to change the world—through your purchases, through your work setting business strategies, and through getting in the trenches within your firm to create impact. It's a big world out there, with big opportunity. Go find your passion, and work to turn your vision into reality.

Acknowledgments

I WANT TO thank all those who lent their knowledge, experience, and support in the creation of this publication. First and foremost, to my family at Nest and my brand colleagues in Responsible Sourcing and Corporate Social Responsibility: thank you for the countless hours you have spent with me and your generosity of spirit in sharing your experiences. I hope that you find these pages a testament to the hard and important work that you are doing each and every day. Thank you also to my colleagues at the NYU Stern School of Business: to Robert Salomon for opening my eyes to the joys of teaching, and to Tensie Whelan and Bruce Buchanan for your tireless efforts to show that business ethics is not just a required class you take as you enter an MBA Program. To Brooke Carey for your help in organizing my thoughts for this book—if you are ever in need of a thought partner, seek Brooke out. And finally, to my family: You are the reason this book is possible. Your support in both the writing of this book and the pursuit of my greater involvement in the intersection between business and impact is a debt that I strive to repay every day. To my wife, Rebecca, for sharing this wonderful life and work with me. Thank you from the bottom of my heart. And to my children, Ella and Sawyer, it is because of you that I fight for a better future.

About the Author

Christopher van Bergen is an adjunct professor at the Leonard N. Stern School of Business at NYU, a lecturer, and business consultant around the country, teaching coursework on social impact and sustainability in business.

Chris is also the CFO/COO of Nest, a nonprofit working in the handworker economy to generate global workforce inclusivity, improve worker well-being beyond factories, and preserve cultural traditions, using radical transparency, data-driven development, and fair market access to connect craftspeople, brands, and consumers in a circular and human-centric value chain.

He helped spearhead Nest's revolutionary compliance program for homework production and oversees Nest's programming, which includes partnerships with pioneering brands from luxury fashion houses to $100B+ retail operations, as well as Nest's business training and mentorship of over 2,000 artisan businesses across 120 countries and strategic initiatives to solve universal sector challenges.

Chris received an Executive MBA from the Leonard N. Stern School of Business at NYU, specializing in global business, strategy, and leadership. He also holds music degrees from the Eastman School of Music and Northwestern University, and a degree in psychology from the University of Rochester.

Endnotes

Chapter 1

1. https://www.buildanest.org/the-nest-seal/ethicalhandcraft/.
2. Nest State of the Handworker Economy Report, 2019. https://www.buildanest.org/wp-content/uploads/2019/05/Nest-State-of-the-Handworker-Economy-Report-2019.pdf.
3. UN Women, Commission on the Status of Women, 2012. https://www.unwomen.org/en/news/in-focus/commission-on-the-status-of-women-2012/facts-and-figures.
4. https://www.macrotrends.net/countries/PHL/philippines/inflation-rate-cpi.

Chapter 2

1. Bentz, Bridget, Molly Seavy-Nesper, and Gisele Grayson. "How 'modern-day slavery' in the Congo powers the rechargeable battery economy." Article based on interview in *Fresh Air* podcast, hosted by Terry Gross, February 1, 2023. https://www.npr.org/sections/goatsandsoda/2023/02/01/1152893248/red-cobalt-congo-drc-mining-siddharth-kara.

2. Friedman, Milton. "A Friedman doctrine—The Social Responsibility of Business Is to Increase Its Profits", The New York Times, September 13, 1970. https://www.nytimes.com/1970/09/13/archives/a-friedman-doctrine-the-social-responsibility-of-business-is-to.html.

3. https://worldsmostethicalcompanies.com/honorees/.

4. Sisodia, Rajendra, David Wolfe, et al. *Firms of Endearment: How World-Class Companies Profit from Passion and Purpose.* Pearson Education, 2014.

5. Collins, Jim. *Good to Great: Why Some Companies Make the Leap and Others Don't.* Harper Business, 2001.

6. Ferran, David, and Katy Sperry. "Do Company Ethics and Stakeholder Focus Equal Greater Long-Run Shareholder Profits?" The Torrey Project, September 19, 2022. https://www.torreyproject.org/post/ethics-stakeholder-focus-greater-long-run-shareholder-profits.

7. https://customfabricflowers.com/about/history/.

8. https://www.nyc.gov/assets/planning/download/pdf/data-maps/nyc-population/historical-population/nyc_total_pop_1900-2010.pdf.

9. https://ilgwu.ilr.cornell.edu/history/.

10. https://www.pbs.org/wgbh/americanexperience/features/biography-clara-lemlich/.

11. Villarreal, M. Angeles and Ian Fergusson. *The North American Free Trade Agreement (NAFTA)* Congressional Research Service, May 24, 2017, p. 21.

12. Fernández Campbell, Alexia. "Nearly 5 Million U.S. Jobs Depend on Trade With Mexico." The Atlantic, December 9, 2016. https://www.theatlantic.com/business/archive/2016/12/mexico-nafta-trade/510008/.

13. Chatzky, Andrew, James McBride, and Mohammed Aly Sergie. "NAFTA and the USMCA: Weighing the Impact of North American Trade." Council on Foreign Relations, July 1, 2020. https://www.cfr.org/backgrounder/naftas-economic-impact.

14. Scott, Robert. "Heading South: U.S.-Mexico trade and job displacement after NAFTA." Economic Policy Institute, May 3, 2011. https://www.epi.org/publication/heading_south_u-s-mexico_trade_and_job_displacement_after_nafta1/.

15. Thomas, Dana. "Is This Small Town the Future of Ethical Fashion?" The Cut, September 9, 2019. https://www.thecut.com/2019/09/is-florence-alabama-the-future-of-ethical-fashion.html.

16. https://journal.alabamachanin.com/2013/10/the-heart-the-factory/.

17. https://www.citizen.org/article/california-job-loss-during-the-nafta-wto-period/.

18. Amadeo, Kimberly. "The Problems With NAFTA." The Balance, updated January 20, 2022. https://www.thebalancemoney.com/disadvantages-of-nafta-3306273.

19. Author unknown. "Michael Jordan Net Worth 2021: What is Jordan's deal with Nike?" Marca.com, October 17, 2021. https://www.marca.com/en/basketball/nba/2021/10/17/616c0df146163f846f8b45b5.html.

20. Peterson, Hayley. "One Stunning Stat That Shows How Nike Changed the Shoe Industry Forever." Business Insider, April 22, 2014. https://www.businessinsider.com/how-nike-changed-the-shoe-industry-2014-4.

21. Davis, Gerald. *The Vanishing American Corporation: Navigating the Hazards of a New Economy*. Berrett-Koehler Publishers, Inc., 2016.

22. Meyer, Jack. "History of Nike: Timeline and Facts." TheStreet.com, August 14, 2019. https://www.thestreet.com/lifestyle/history-of-nike-15057083.

23. Ballinger, Jeffrey. "The New Free-Trade Heel: Nike's profits jump on the backs of Asian workers." *Harper's Magazine*, August 1992. http://archive.harpers.org/1992/08/pdf/HarpersMagazine-1992-08-0000971.pdf.

24. Schanberg, Sydney. "Six Cents an Hour." *Life* magazine, March 28, 1996. https://laborrights.org/in-the-news/six-cents-hour-1996-life-article.

25. Ibid.

26. Author unknown. "Nike doesn't take comic strip's message on sweatshops standing still." *Tampa Bay Times*, June 7, 1997. https://www.tampabay.com/archive/1997/06/07/nike-doesn-t-take-comic-strip-s-message-on-sweatshops-standing-still/.

27. Stolle, Dietlind and Michele Micheletti. *Political Consumerism: Global Responsibility in Action*. Cambridge University Press, 2013, p. 178.

28. https://www.imdb.com/title/tt0124295/.

29. Hendrix, Anastasia. "Fans outnumber protesters at NikeTown." SF Gate, February 23, 1997. https://www.sfgate.com/bayarea/article/Fans-outnumber-protesters-at-NikeTown-3133497.php.

30. Cushman, Jr., John. "Nike Pledges to End Child Labor and Apply U.S. Rules Abroad." *The New York Times*, May 13, 1998. https://www.nytimes.com/1998/05/13/business/international-business-nike-pledges-to-end-child-labor-and-apply-us-rules-abroad.html.

31. http://www.nikecirculardesign.com/.

32. McKenna, Beth. "If You Invested $1,000 in Nike's IPO, This Is the Staggering Amount of Money You'd Have Now." The Motley Fool, February 24, 2020. https://www.fool.com/investing/2020/02/24/if-you-invested-1000-in-nikes-ipo-this-is-the-stag.aspx.

Chapter 3

1. https://ourworldindata.org/internet.

2. Ryan, Tom. "Will consumers ever get over the price hurdle for sustainable goods?" RetailWire.com, December 9, 2021. https://retailwire.com/discussion/will-consumers-ever-get-over-the-price-hurdle-for-sustainable-goods/.

3. Kronthal-Sacco, Randi, and Tensie Whelan. "Sustainable Market Share Index: Research on 2015–2020 IRI Purchasing Data Reveals Sustainability Drives Growth, Survives the Pandemic." NYU Stern Center for Sustainable Business, July 16, 2020. https://www.stern.nyu.edu/sites/default/files/assets/documents/NYU%20Stern%20CSB%20Sustainable%20Market%20Share%20Index%202020.pdf.

4. https://engageforgood.com/portern-novelli-cone-genz-2019/.

5. Kell, Georg. "The Remarkable Rise Of ESG." Forbes.com, July 11, 2018. https://www.forbes.com/sites/georgkell/2018/07/11/the-remarkable-rise-of-esg/?sh=300f50041695.

6. Author unknown. "Triple bottom line." *The Economist, November* 17, 2009. https://www.economist.com/news/2009/11/17/triple-bottom-line.

7. Pérez, Luxy, Dame Vivian Hunt, Hamid Samandari et al. "Does ESG really matter—and why?" McKinsey.com, August 10, 2022. https://www.mckinsey.com/capabilities/sustainability/our-insights/does-esg-really-matter-and-why.

8. https://www.blackrock.com/americas-offshore/en/larry-fink-ceo-letter.

9. Nishant, Niket, and Mehr Bedi. "Louisiana to remove $794 Mln from BlackRock funds over ESG drive." Reuters.com, October 5, 2022. https://www.reuters.com/business/sustainable-business/louisiana-remove-794-mln-blackrock-funds-over-esg-drive-2022-10-05/.

10. Wilner, Tamar. "Puma Reveals 'World's First' Environmental P&L Results." Environmentalleader.com, May 16, 2011. https://www.environmentalleader.com/2011/05/puma-reveals-worlds-first-environmental-pl-results/.

11. https://www.puma-catchup.com/pumas-environmental-impacts-decrease-15-since-2013/.

12. https://www.theclimatepledge.com/.

13. https://www.qualtrics.com/blog/company-values-employee-retention/.

14. https://sustainability.williams-sonomainc.com/2022/03/09/wsi-celebrates-international-womens-day-in-partnership-with-nest-ethical-handcraft-program/.

15. https://unglobalcompact.org/library/4451.

16. Miebach, Michael. "Sharing accountability and success: Why we're linking employee compensation to ESG goals." Mastercard.com/news, April 19, 2022. https://www.mastercard.com/news/perspectives/2022/esg-goals-and-employee-compensation/.

Chapter 4

1. https://www.isealalliance.org/.
2. https://apparelcoalition.org/the-sac/.
3. Shendruk, Amanda. "The controversial way fashion brands gauge sustainability is being suspended." Qz.com, June 29, 2022. https://qz.com/2180322/the-controversial-higg-sustainability-index-is-being-suspended.
4. Tabuchi, Hiroko. "How Fashion Giants Recast Plastic as Good for the Planet." *The New York Times*, June 12, 2022. https://www.nytimes.com/2022/06/12/climate/vegan-leather-synthetics-fashion-industry.html.
5. Author unknown. "Why You Should Be Paying Attention to What's Happening with the Higg Material Sustainability Index." Fibershed.com, August 17, 2022. https://fibershed.org/2022/08/17/why-you-should-be-paying-attention-to-whats-happening-with-the-higg-index/.

Chapter 5

1. https://www.ilo.org/global/topics/geip/WCMS_614394/lang--en/index.htm.
2. Yardley, Jim. "Report on Deadly Factory Collapse in Bangladesh Finds Widespread Blame." *The New York Times*, May 22, 2013. https://www.nytimes.com/2013/05/23/world/asia/report-on-bangladesh-building-collapse-finds-widespread-blame.html.
3. Author unknown. "Brands risk image in varying Bangladesh responses." Usatoday.com, May 6, 2013. https://www.usatoday.com/story/news/world/2013/05/06/brands-risk-image-in-varying-bangladesh-responses/2138299/.
4. Young, Sarah. "Fashion Revolution Week: What was the Rana Plaza disaster and why did it happen?" The Independent, April 23, 2020. https://www.independent.co.uk/life-style/fashion/rana-plaza-factory-disaster-anniversary-what-happened-fashion-a9478126.html.

5. https://www.govinfo.gov/content/pkg/CPRT-113SPRT85633/html/CPRT-113SPRT85633.htm.

6. Ovi, Ibrahim Hossain. "RMG export defiant against all odds." *Dhaka Tribune,* July 12, 2013. https://archive.dhakatribune.com/uncategorized/2013/07/12/rmg-export-defiant-against-all-odds.

7. https://hmgroup.com/wp-content/uploads/2020/11/Conscious-Actions-Sustainability-Report-2012.pdf, p. 40.

8. https://www.govinfo.gov/content/pkg/CPRT-113SPRT85633/html/CPRT-113SPRT85633.htm.

9. Holland, Tiffany. "Bangladesh tragedy won't affect most shoppers' fashion decisions." RetailWeek.com, May 14, 2013. https://www.retail-week.com/bangladesh-tragedy-wont-affect-most-shoppers-fashion-decisions/5049105.article?authent=1.

10. Khazan, Olga. "Better Safety in Bangladesh Could Raise Clothing Prices by About 25 Cents." *The Atlantic,* May 10, 2013. https://www.theatlantic.com/international/archive/2013/05/better-safety-in-bangladesh-could-raise-clothing-prices-by-about-25-cents/275765/.

11. https://bangladeshaccord.org/.

12. Polk, Andy. "Alliance For Bangladesh Worker Safety Update." Footwear Distributors & Retailers of America, October 23, 2014. https://fdra.org/latest-news/alliance-for-bangladesh-worker-safety-update/.

13. Roberts, Alan. "The Bangladesh Accord factory audits finds more than 80,000 safety hazards." *The Guardian,* October 15, 2014. https://www.theguardian.com/sustainable-business/2014/oct/15/bangladesh-accord-factory-hazards-protect-worker-safety-fashion.

14. https://remake.world/stories/payup-two-years-later/.

15. Graceffo, Loretta. "Garment Workers Win $22 Billion in Historic Victory Against Wage Theft." Countercurrents.org, March 26, 2021. https://countercurrents.org/2021/03/garment-workers-win-22-billion-in-historic-victory-against-wage-theft/.

16. Author unknown. "Microsoft Pledges $55 Million in Support of COVID-19 Relief." Philanthropy News Digest, April 14, 2020. https://philanthropynewsdigest.org/news/microsoft-pledges-55-million-in-support-of-covid-19-relief.

17. https://corporate.target.com/about/purpose-history/our-commitments/target-coronavirus-info.
18. Choi, Thomas, Dale Rogers, et al. "Coronavirus Is a Wake-Up Call for Supply Chain Management." *Harvard Business Review*, March 27, 2020.
19. Hyken, Shep. "Selling To Gen-Z: This Is What They Want." *Forbes*, June 12, 2022. https://www.forbes.com/sites/shephyken/2022/06/12/selling-to-gen-z-this-is-what-they-want/?sh=2f61ba0458f5.
20. Amed, Imran, Achim Berg, et al. "The State of Fashion 2021." McKinsey & Company, 2021.
21. www.researchandmarkets.com/reports/4592343/handicrafts-market-global-industry-trends.

Chapter 6

1. Nidumolu, Ram, Jib Ellison, et al. "The Collaboration Imperative." *Harvard Business Review*, April 2014.
2. Fastco Works. "Why strategic partnerships can help brands elevate their social responsibility." Fast Company, May 13, 2022. https://www.fastcompany.com/90750780/why-strategic-partnerships-can-help-brands-elevate-their-social-responsibility.
3. Denning, Steve. "What's Behind Warby Parker's Success?" *Forbes*, March 23, 2016. https://www.forbes.com/sites/stevedenning/2016/03/23/whats-behind-warby-parkers-success/?sh=226c126b411a.
4. Gergen, Christopher and Gregg Vanourek. "Vision(ary) Entrepreneur." *Harvard Business Review*, August 14, 2008. https://hbr.org/2008/08/visionary-entrepreneur.
5. Rojo, Ava. "Warby Parker Celebrates Over 10 Million Pairs of Glasses Distributed Through its Buy a Pair, Give a Pair Program." BusinessWire, February 28, 2022. https://www.businesswire.com/news/home/20220228005812/en/Warby-Parker-Celebrates-Over-10-Million-Pairs-of-Glasses-Distributed-Through-its-Buy-a-Pair-Give-a-Pair-Program.

6. https://mcdonough.com/cradle-to-cradle/.

7. http://www.product-life.org/en/cradle-to-cradle.

8. https://www.manualsdir.com/manuals/254925/herman-miller-mirra-chairs-seating-material-content-and-recyclability.html?page=2.

9. Dorfman, Josh. "The Mirra 2 Chair Elevates Comfort, Design, and Sustainability." Lazyenvironmentalist.com, October 29, 2020. https://lazyenvironmentalist.com/the-mirra-2-chair-comfort-design-sustainability/.

10. Makower, Joel. " Loop's launch brings reusable packaging to the world's biggest brands." Greenbiz.com, January 24, 2019. https://www.greenbiz.com/article/loops-launch-brings-reusable-packaging-worlds-biggest-brands#:~:text=Along%20the%20way%2C%20the%20company,TerraCycle%20developed%20over%20the%20years.

11. https://sustainbleninja.com/fashion-industry-waste-statistics/.

12. Roberts-Islam, Brooke. "Evrnu's Recycled Waste Fiber Launches Today, And Could Outperform 90% Of Existing Textiles." *Forbes*, April 1, 2022. https://www.forbes.com/sites/brookerobertsislam/2022/04/01/evrnus-recycled-waste-fiber—launches-today-and-could-outperform-90-of-existing-textiles/?sh=6e3754692539.

13. https://www.allbirds.com/pages/allbirds-adidas-futurecraft-collaboration.

14. Bousquet, Carol. "New Balance says its sneakers will leave zero carbon footprint by 2050." Mainepublic.org, April 12, 2022. https://www.mainepublic.org/environment-and-outdoors/2022-04-12/carbon-footprint-new-balance-says-its-sneakers-will-have-net-zero-emissions-by-2050.

15. https://ulula.com/.

16. https://sourcemap.com/.

17. https://www.hyperledger.org/learn/publications/walmart-case-study.

18. https://www.banqu.co/.

Chapter 7

1. Neate, Rupert. "Yvon Chouinard—the 'existential dirtbag' who founded and gifted Patagonia." *The Guardian*, September 15, 2022. https://www.theguardian.com/global/2022/sep/15/yvon-chouinard-the-existential-dirtbag-who-founded-and-gifted-patagonia.

2. Collings, Richard. "Patagonia's valuation likely more than $4.5B." Axios.com, October 3, 2022. https://www.axios.com/pro/retail-deals/2022/10/03/patagonias-valuation-likely-more-than-45b.

3. https://www.patagonia.com/stories/product-testing-4/story-20158.html.

4. Chouinard, Yvon. *Let My People Go Surfing: The Education of a Reluctant Businessman*. Penguin Books, 2016, p. 200.

5. https://www.patagonia.com/stories/dont-buy-this-jacket-black-friday-and-the-new-york-times/story-18615.html.

6. Segran, Elizabeth. "Patagonia has had enormous success with upcycled clothing. Could other brands follow?" *Fast Company*, January 11, 2021. https://www.fastcompany.com/90592541/patagonia-has-had-enormous-success-with-upcycled-clothing-could-other-brands-follow.

7. https://www.patagonia.com/stories/our-quest-for-circularity/story-96496.html.

8. https://www.patagonia.com/stories/environmental-c/story-20285.html.

9. https://www.patagonia.com/our-footprint/working-with-factories.html.

10. https://www.patagoniaworks.com/press/2022/9/14/patagonias-next-chapter-earth-is-now-our-only-shareholder.

11. https://www.patagonia.com/stories/freedom-through-fabric/story-121919.html.

12. Heller, Matthew. "A Firm Tries to Be Itself While Getting Bigger." Reuters News, January 11, 1989.

13. Neate, Rupert. "Yvon Chouinard—the 'existential dirtbag' who founded and gifted Patagonia." *The Guardian*, September 15,

2022. https://www.theguardian.com/global/2022/sep/15/yvon-chouinard-the-existential-dirtbag-who-founded-and-gifted-patagonia.

14. Gunther, Marc. "The Patagonia Adventure: Yvon Chouinard's Stubborn Desire to Redefine Business." Bthechange.com, September 6, 2016. https://bthechange.com/the-patagonia-adven ture-yvon-chouinards-stubborn-desire-to-redefine-business-f60f7ab8dd60.

15. Maheshwari, Sapna. "Patagonia, Quick to Close, Could Be Last to Reopen." *The New York Times,* May 12, 2020. https://www .nytimes.com/2020/05/12/business/patagonia-reopening-coronavirus.html.

16. Salpini, Cara. "Patagonia CEO Rose Marcario steps down." Retaildive.com, June 11, 2020. https://www.retaildive.com/news/ patagonia-ceo-rose-marcario-steps-down/579648/.

17. Cerullo, Megan. "Patagonia will no longer sell vests with finance firm logos on them." CBS News, April 3, 2019. https://www .cbsnews.com/news/midtown-uniform-patagonia-will-no-longer-sell-vests-with-finance-firms-logos-on-them/.

18. https://www.linkedin.com/pulse/unique-challenges-running-patagonia-ceo-ryan-gellert-talks-roth/.

19. https://www.unilever.com/brands/.

20. https://companiesmarketcap.com/unilever/marketcap/.

21. https://www.unilever.com/news/news-search/2020/90-years-of-doing-good-why-companies-with-purpose-last/.

22. Unilever Charts 2014. https://www.unilever.com/files/origin/da80a 49d6fd-382c0e3efe463cce88c4b9e3af7f8.pdf/ir_unilever_ charts_2005-2014.pdf.

23. https://www.unilever.com/our-company/our-history-and-archives/ 2010-2020/.

24. Khairunisa, Mutia, and Nazalea Kusuma. "How Unilever Trans-forms Its Business with Unilever Sustainable Living Plan." Green-network.asia, July 9, 2021. https://greennetwork.asia/news/how-unilever-transforms-its-business-with-unilever-sustainable-living-plan/.

25. Koyanagi, Ken. "Unilever CEO values sustainable-development opportunities in Asia." *Nikkei Asian Review,* October 15, 2017. https://asia.nikkei.com/Business/Unilever-CEO-values-sustainable-development-opportunities-in-Asia.

26. Feloni, Richard. "Former Unilever CEO Paul Polman Explains How He's Building a Movement of CEOs to Change How the World Does Business." Just Capital, October 8, 2021. https://justcapital.com/news/former-unilever-ceo-paul-polman-on-net-positive-and-building-a-coalition-of-ceos-to-change-business/.

27. Polman, Paul, and CB Bhattacharya. "Engaging Employees to Create a Sustainable Business." *Stanford Social Innovation Review,* Fall 2016. https://ssir.org/articles/entry/engaging_employees_to_create_a_sustainable_business.

28. https://weinrebgroup.com/wp-content/uploads/2018/07/CSO-Back-Story-II.pdf.

29. Unilever Sustainable Living Plan 2010 to 2020: Summary of 10 years' progress, March 2021. https://www.unilever.com/files/92ui5egz/production/16cb778e4d31b81509dc5937001559f1f5c863ab.pdf.

30. Saunders, Andrew. "The MT Interview: Assuming His New Role in the Midst of a Global Recession." Management Today, March 1, 2011.

31. https://www.youtube.com/watch?v=6pVM1okMN8o.

32. Author unknown. "Unilever and Walmart in joint water saving campaign." Edie.net, October 28, 2011. https://www.edie.net/unilever-and-walmart-in-joint-water-saving-campaign/.

33. Author unknown. "Unilever Sustainable Living Plan 2010 to 2020: Summary of 10 years' progress." March 2021. https://www.unilever.com/files/92ui5egz/production/16cb778e4d31b81509dc5937001559f1f5c863ab.pdf.

34. https://www.mastercardcenter.org/.

35. Brennan, Joe. "After its 'near-death experience,' where does Unilever go from here?" *The Irish Times,* January 21, 2022. https://www.irishtimes.com/business/markets/after-its-near-death-experience-where-does-unilever-go-from-here-1.4782499.

Chapter 8

1. Kronthal-Sacco, Randi, and Tensie Whelan. "Sustainable Market Share Index: 2021 Report." NYU Stern Center for Sustainable Business, updated April 2022. https://www.stern.nyu.edu/sites/default/files/assets/documents/FINAL%202021%20CSB%20Practice%20Forum%20website_0.pdf.

2. Newman, Daniel. "How Leading Global Companies Are Using Sustainability As A Market Differentiator." *Forbes*, July 24, 2020. https://www.forbes.com/sites/danielnewman/2020/07/24/how-leading-global-companies-are-using-sustainability-as-a-market-differentiator/?sh=5fe51f731ff3.

3. Maheshwari, Sapna. "Sephora Signs '15 Percent Pledge' to Carry More Black-Owned Brands." *The New York Times*, June 10, 2020. https://www.nytimes.com/2020/06/10/business/sephora-black-owned-brands.html.

4. MacLeod, Scott. "Sustainability-Focused Marketing is Increasingly Under the Microscope." AdvertisingWeek.com, 2021. https://advertisingweek.com/sustainability-focused-marketing-is-increasingly-under-the-microscope/.

5. Testa, Jessica, Vanessa Friedman, and Elizabeth Paton. "Everlane's Promsie of 'Radical Transparency' Unravels." *The New York Times*, July 26, 2020.

6. Mustafa, Alifiya. "Everlane—An eCommerce That Grew From $0 to $100M+ in 6 years!" Pixelphant.com, November 28, 2022. https://pixelphant.com/blog/ecomstories-everlane-ecommerce.

7. Rodríguez Vilá, Omar and Sundar Bharadwaj. "Competing on Social Purpose." *Harvard Business Review*, September-October 2017.

8. https://www.youtube.com/watch?v=o9l9UiIR26Y.

9. https://www.youtube.com/watch?v=bReBO55XzZc.

10. Spangler, Todd. "Adam McKay's Scathing Fake Chevron Ad Blasting Its Role in Climate Change Goes Viral." Variety.com, September 30, 2022. https://variety.com/2022/digital/news/adam-mckay-fake-chevron-ad-viral-1235389355/.

11. https://nisolo.com/blogs/stride-sustainability/the-lowest-wage-in-our-supply-chain.

12. Fleming, Molly. "Consumers Don't Want to Choose Between Sustainability and Convenience." Marketing Week, February 26, 2020.

13. Huntsdale, Justin. "Majority of Nespresso coffee pods heading to landfill as company ramps up recycling message." Abc.net.au, November 15, 2019. https://www.abc.net.au/news/2019-11-16/most-nespresso-coffee-pods-not-being-recycled/11708910.

14. Segal, Mark. "UK Regulator to Test Asset Managers' ESG Claims for Greenwashing." ESGtoday.com, February 7, 2023. https://www.esgtoday.com/uk-regulator-to-test-asset-managers-esg-claims-for-greenwashing/.

15. https://www.sec.gov/news/press-release/2022-86.

16. https://www.buildinggreen.com/about.

17. https://www.buildinggreen.com/news-article/nine-types-greenwashing.

18. Statt, Nick. "Allbirds tells Amazon it forgot to steal the most important part of its shoe." Theverge.com, November 25, 2019. https://www.theverge.com/2019/11/25/20982653/allbirds-ceo-amazon-copy-shoe-environment-sustainability-steal.

19. https://www.buildinggreen.com/news-article/nine-types-greenwashing.

20. Hunt, Katie. "Here's how many times you need to reuse your reusable grocery bags." Cnn.com, March 13, 2023. https://www.cnn.com/2022/12/13/world/cotton-tote-vs-plastic-bags-environment-climate-cost-scn/index.html.

21. Wei, Brandon. "Environmental groups fight greenwashing in forestry 'sustainability' certification scheme." Greenpeace.org, December 2, 2022. https://www.greenpeace.org/canada/en/press-release/55547/environmental-groups-fight-greenwashing-in-forestry-sustainability-certification-scheme/.

22. Delmas, Magali A. and Vanessa Cuerel Burbano. "The Drivers of Greenwashing." California Management Review, Fall 2011.

23. The Economist Intelligence Unit. "An Eco-wakening: Measuring global awareness, engagement and action for nature." *The Economist*, 2021. https://files.worldwildlife.org/wwfcmsprod/files/Publication/file/93ts5bhvyq_An_EcoWakening_Measuring_awareness__engagement_and_action_for_nature_FINAL_MAY_2021.pdf?_ga=2.58501802.1646844832.1675726401-621447303.1675726400.

24. D'Addario, Daniel. "Why the Kendall Jenner Pepsi Ad Was Such a Glaring Misstep." *Time*, April 5, 2017. https://time.com/4726500/pepsi-ad-kendall-jenner/.

Chapter 9

1. https://marcopolonetwork.com/evolution-of-trade-finance-blockchain/.
2. https://usa.bnpparibas/en/the-new-economics-of-supply-chain-sustainability/.
3. https://rootcapital.org/wp-content/uploads/2022/02/2021-QPR-Q4.pdf.
4. https://rootcapital.org/impact_areas/livelihoods/.
5. https://rootcapital.org/impact_areas/livelihoods/.
6. https://www.accion.org/mastercard-accion-partnering-inclusive-growth.
7. Biondi, Annachiara. "Prada is first in industry to sign sustainability-linked loan." Vogue Business, November 5, 2019. https://www.voguebusiness.com/sustainability/prada-launches-sustainability-linked-loan.
8. https://blog.google/alphabet/alphabet-issues-sustainability-bonds-support-environmental-and-social-initiatives/.
9. Whelan, Tensie, and Elyse Douglas. "How to Talk to Your CFO About Sustainability." *Harvard Business Review*, January-February 2021. https://hbr.org/2021/01/how-to-talk-to-your-cfo-about-sustainability.

10. Rifkin, Sophie, Rithu Raman et al. "The Business Case for Sustainable Apparel at EILEEN FISHER." NYU Stern Center for Sustainable Business, January, 2021. https://www.stern.nyu.edu/ sites/default/files/assets/documents/EILEEN%20FISHER%20 Case.pdf.

Chapter 10

1. Proctor, James. "Transforming a Hero Culture." The Inteq Group, 2014. https://www.inteqgroup.com/blog/transforming-a-hero-culture#:~:text=A%20%E2%80%9Chero%20culture%E2% 80%9D%20is%20an,sheer%20strength%2C%20will%20and% 20knowledge.
2. https://www.ted.com/talks/lorna_davis_a_guide_to_ collaborative_leadership?language=en.

Index

Bangladesh Fire and Safety Accord, 93–94
Bangladesh Garment Manufacturers for Export Association (BGMEA), auditing responsibility, 89
BanQu, 193–194
  financial transactions mapping, 122
B Corp, 63
  certification, 73, 199
  status, 144
Benchmarking, 141–142
Better Cotton initiatives, 118
Big One, The (Knight), 29
Black, Indigenous, and People of Color (BIPOC) businesses
  financial support, 101
  shelf space, leveraging, 170
  makers, 182
Black Lives Matter Movement, 30, 101, 169, 194
Blackrock
  responsibility, increase, 98
  sustainability-related disclosures, 41–42
Blockchain-based solutions, impact, 120–121
Blockchain technology, usage, 57, 121–122
Blood diamonds, sourcing, 167
Blumenthal, Neil, 112–113
BNP Paribas (financing partner), 179–180, 183
BNY Mellon, Investment Adviser business (payments), 162
Board of directors
  corporate responsibility, 43–46
  system, success, 47
  positive change, creation, 47

Body scanning technology, usage, 196
Brands
  brand-to-brand collaboration, 117–118
  claims, problems, 165
  competitor knowledge, 108–109
  contractor payments, 96
  cost emphasis, problems, 91
  definition, absence, 165
  design team, impact, 48
  distribution, 177
  downstream role, 11
  life cycle, avoidance, 165–166
  messaging, 153
  NGO cost/partnering sharing, 78
  non sequitur, 165
  overpromises, issues, 38
  proclamation, 165–166
  public declarations, issues, 46–47
  relationships/trust/insight, failure, 50
  reputation, risk, 121
  shock preparedness, 98–99
  standards, 63–64
  success, stories, 127
  supplier code of conduct, following, 5
  systems, success, 39
  value messaging, 152–155
  visibility, need, 36–37
  weaknesses, exposure/overcoming, 90–93
Braungart, Michael, 114, 203
Buildinggreen.com, 164–165
Bureau Veritas, 67, 107
Business
  education, standard-setting bodies (focus), 71–72
  finance, 175